SUZANNE MULHOLLAND

BATCH FROM SCRATCH

SAVE MONEY AND TIME
WITH THIS 28-DAY MEAL PLAN

To all the families who opened their doors and allowed us to show the nation how to batch cook from their kitchens, and to everyone who has viewed the show, a huge thank you.

CONTENTS

4 Introduction
6 What is Batch from Scratch?
7 The Principles of Batching
8 Toolkit
10 How the Recipes Work
14 Refrigerating, Freezing, Defrosting and Reheating
16 Batching on a Budget
18 Meal Planning

20 MEAL PLANNER
44 BREAKFASTS
56 LUNCHES
86 DINNERS

124 Conversion Tables
125 Index
127 Thanks

INTRODUCTION

If you've ever stood in the kitchen at 5:15pm, fridge door open, stomach rumbling, with absolutely no idea what to cook then you're not alone. Let's be honest, so many of us dread that daily question: 'What's for dinner?' That is exactly where this book comes in. *Batch from Scratch* isn't just a recipe book; it's a lifeline for busy lives, a solution for stressed-out mealtimes, and a big comforting hug for anyone who just wants dinner to be easier.

This book is designed to help you finally feel in control of what's going on in your kitchen, without overwhelm or stress. It gives you a chance to have a reset and start living the life you want, where you feel in control of mealtimes AND your food budget. You'll learn how to plan what to eat for the week ahead, how to shop smarter to save money and how to cook smarter to save time. Welcome to the world of batching!

The recipes inside are mostly taken from series 1 of the Channel 4 show, with a few from series 2 making an appearance. They are comforting, easy to follow, low cost and focused on the kind of food we *actually* eat at home, with recipes for breakfasts, lunches and main meals. All the recipes have been amalgamated into four weekly meal plans, although you can also choose to make your own personalised plan to suit your family's needs by combining your own family favourites with recipes from the book using the interactive meal plan on pages 37–40.

All the dinner recipes and most of the lunch and breakfast recipes are freezable, so you can get ahead of the game and cook when you want to, not when you have to. This is the essence of batching from scratch! You'll find a super straightforward step-by-step guide to walk you through the basics: freezing, defrosting, portioning and even labelling your bags so you don't lose your mind hunting for the mystery meal in the freezer (see pages 14–15). Grab a cuppa and flick through the pages that follow; in five minutes, you'll have learned a whole new life skill. I promise it's that simple, whether you're meal-prepping for one, feeding a hungry family of four, or somewhere in between. This isn't about perfection. It's about making things that little bit easier, one meal at a time. Watch your shopping bills and your stress decrease while your health and bank balance increase as you follow along on the batch from scratch journey.

Let's batch – from scratch!

INTRODUCTION

WHAT IS BATCH FROM SCRATCH?

Batch from Scratch: Cooking for Less is a hit Channel 4 show presented by Suzanne Mulholland – aka The Batch Lady – and Joe Swash. The show helps struggling households from around the country who find mealtimes a daily battle. Suzanne and Joe analyse every meal eaten, every minute wasted and every pound spent. Along with clever hacks and monthly meal plans, they successfully cut costs, save time and create easy batch-cooked meals for the freezer, giving each family a great new routine when it comes to putting food on the table.

This book gives you a chance to experience all the top tips, hacks, recipes and meal plans from the show. It's been created to help you achieve the same end goals. You can make the recipes, discover how to freeze and defrost meals and learn how to create your own meal plans specifically personalised for your family. If you ever wanted Joe and Suzanne to jump out of the TV and help you to slash your food bill, free up valuable time and batch-cook and freeze multiple meals, then this is the book for you.

Since the show launched in February 2025 it has had huge success with over 1 million viewers tuning in each week, proving that batch-cooking isn't just a clever hack, it's a lifestyle shift.

Want to rewatch series 1 or 2 of *Batch from Scratch*? Remember you can stream the show on Channel 4's streaming channel or through the app.

Batch from Scratch is a Channel 4 show
Co-created by Suzanne Mulholland (The Batch Lady Ltd) and Southshore Productions Ltd
Produced by Southshore Productions Ltd
Sponsored by Lidl
Presented by Suzanne Mulholland and Joe Swash.

THE PRINCIPLES OF BATCHING

BATCH

/ verb

to group items for speedy processing:

i.e. Let's batch meals for the week ahead!

Batch-cooking isn't just about saving time in the kitchen; it also saves time on all the related chores like planning, shopping and washing up.

Streamline your shopping

Batching has so many benefits. By simply doing a small amount of planning at the beginning of the week (i.e. 5–10 minutes with a cuppa) you can streamline your shopping so that you buy all the food for the week ahead in one go. You instantly know what you're eating that week, thus reducing food waste and multiple trips to the shops.

Double bubble!

The average UK family generally eats the same 7–10 meals on rotation, with a few new recipes, takeaways or nights out sprinkled throughout those 7–10 meals. So, as we eat on rotation why not cook on rotation too? It takes about 20 minutes to make a spaghetti bolognese for four people, but it only takes 5 minutes extra to make double the amount. If you start to cook with the mindset of 'one for now, one for later', you create a stock of extra meals that only took you 5 minutes to prepare. Better still, that meal is sitting ready for you in the freezer, giving you a whole night off from cooking and clearing up.

Same base, different meal

If you follow the meal plans, you'll see that some nights you double up the quantities so you have one meal one night with another to go into the freezer to be had a few weeks later. Another great hack you'll also learn is to serve that extra freezer meal a different way: for example, if the first time it was chilli with rice, the next time you can serve it as chilli nachos.

Your freezer is your friend

Freezers really don't get as much credit as they should, but they are brilliant! They allow food to be kept for a long time using NO artificial additives – just good old-fashioned ice. Think of your freezer as your TV remote control: you can make a meal, then press pause (by putting the meal in the freezer) and come back any time you like to enjoy it. Exactly like pausing your favourite TV show to watch another day. The freezer allows you to cook when you want and eat when you want, without needing to cook from scratch every night.

The next few pages will guide you through everything you need to know about batching, freezing and defrosting. It really is super simple.

Suzanne x

TOOLKIT

You don't need a lot to start batching! The freezer bags and marker pens are the essentials (recommended styles and sizes can be found on thebatchlady.com).

Reusable freezer bags allow you to freeze all your meals flat and can be used over and over. Keep small and large options to batch different portion sizes or for recipes that require some foods to be stored separately.

Baggie holders to keep your freezer bag open as you fill it.

Ovenproof dish with plastic lid. Pyrex freezer-to-oven glass dishes with plastic sealable lids are perfect.
- For 4 people: 2.6-litre ovenproof dish
- For 2 people: 1.3–1.5-litre ovenproof dish

Sharpie pens for writing on plastic bags or tubs. Although this doesn't wash off, just score out and write below old writing if reusing the bag.

Kitchen foil for protecting food in the oven or air fryer. Don't buy catering foil as it's too thick and stops the cooking process.

Chalk marker pens for writing on reusable bags – they wash off easily.

Measuring cups and spoons. If you want to work fast, ditch the scales and use measuring cups – I give both options in my recipes. The cup should be filled to the brim but not heaped.

Cup sizes differ slightly between countries, above shows the cup sizes used throughout this book.

¼ cup / 60ml / 4 tbsp
½ cup / 120ml / 8 tbsp
1 cup / 240ml / 16 tbsp

Plastic freezer bags in different sizes are ideal for food that would stain reusable bags. Although these are plastic, they can be washed out and reused.

Scrub Mommy sponge for washing out freezer bags, with a soft side and abrasive side.

- **For 4 people:** 2.5-litre bag
- **For 2 people:** 1.2-litre bag
- **For 1 person:** 600ml bag

(based on average freezer bags, sizes will vary dependent on shape)

TOOLKIT

HOW THE RECIPES WORK

There are two different kinds of recipes in this book: 'Grab and Cook' recipes, which are frozen raw, ready for you to cook when you need them, and 'Cook Ahead' recipes, cooked prior to freezing.

Grab and Cook Recipes

These recipes are very quick to make, as no cooking occurs before freezing. The Grab and Cook recipes in this book use a colour-coded block system. You have the choice to make it ahead for the fridge or the freezer (follow the blue instructions) or to make it to eat now (follow the red instructions).

SPATCHCOCK SUNDAY CHICKEN

A delicious, easy way to enjoy a roast chicken – serve with gravy and some Yorkshire puddings!

Prep: 10 minutes | **Cook:** 1 hour | **Serves:** 4

GRAB AND COOK

- 1 large whole chicken
- 2 tsp dried rosemary
- 1 tsp dried thyme
- 1 tsp garlic purée
- 3 tbsp olive oil
- 400g baby carrots
- 2 onions, diced into chunks
- salt and pepper

❄ IF MAKING AHEAD FOR THE FRIDGE OR FREEZER

1. To spatchcock the chicken, turn it upside down with the legs pointing towards you. Using extra sharp scissors, cut down each side of the backbone, through the ribs and right to the end, then remove the backbone.
2. Turn the chicken back over, skin-side up, and open it out. Using the palm of your hand, push the chicken down firmly so that it flattens.
3. Add the rosemary, thyme, garlic, olive oil and salt and pepper to a bowl and mix. Spread this all over the chicken.
4. Add the carrots and onions to a large labelled freezer bag, then add the chicken and seal. Place in the freezer.

OVEN

Remove from the freezer and leave to fully defrost. Once defrosted, preheat the oven to 190°C/170°C fan, pour the carrots and onions onto a tray, then lay the chicken on top. Cook for 1 hour–1 hour 10 minutes until the chicken is cooked through.

AIR FRYER

Remove from the freezer and leave to fully defrost. Once defrosted, preheat the air fryer to 180°C, pour the carrots and onions onto a tray, then lay the chicken on top. Cook for 50 minutes–1 hour until the chicken is cooked through.

IF COOKING NOW

Follow the method for 'if making ahead' until the end of step 3.

OVEN

Preheat the oven to 190°C/170°C fan, pour the carrots and onions onto a tray, then lay the chicken on top. Cook for 1 hour–1 hour 10 minutes until the chicken is cooked through.

AIR FRYER

Preheat the air fryer to 180°C, pour the carrots and onions onto a tray, then lay the chicken on top. Cook for 50 minutes–1 hour until the chicken is cooked through.

Follow these instructions to make the recipe ahead of time. The cooking instructions will also be under blue headings and will show you either how to cook from frozen, or how to defrost and then cook if that is required.

Follow these instructions to make the recipe to eat right away. The cooking instructions are based on the recipe being cooked from fresh, rather than frozen or refrigerated first.

For air-fryer recipes a large-drawered air fryer will be required, or you will have to divide the recipes to fit your air fryer.

From this

EASY TO CUSTOMISE

PORTION-CONTROLLED

PERFECT WHEN BUSY

PREPPED IN ADVANCE

QUICK TO MAKE

CONVENIENT TO COOK

FREES UP HEADSPACE

HELPFUL FOR ANYONE WITH MOBILITY OR DEXTERITY ISSUES

FREE OF ULTRA-PROCESSED FOODS

AVOIDS FOOD WASTE

SAVES ON ENERGY BILLS

To this

HOW THE RECIPES WORK

11

Cook Ahead Recipes

Some of the recipes are designed for you to cook the food first, or cook elements of the recipe first, then freeze it – I call these Cook Ahead recipes. In these recipes you are always given two cooking options, so simply decide what section to follow based on your preferred cooking appliance. Cook the recipes according to the instructions, then leave to cool and pack up in a freezer bag or freezer-proof dish to use later.

Choose your cooking appliance and follow the correct column.

These symbols will help you identify the vegetarian (V) or vegan (VE) recipes in the book.

Occasionally you will see a green or yellow bubble on the page that will offer you alternatives to turn a recipe into a vegetarian or vegan recipe by changing a few of the ingredients.

Follow the cooking instructions for your appliance when ready to cook.

HOW THE RECIPES WORK

Non-freezable Recipes

All the dinner recipes in the book are freezable and most of the lunch and breakfast recipes are too, but there are a few that are not, although they can be made a few days in advance and kept in the fridge. If this is the case, this will be clearly explained in the recipe introduction.

REFRIGERATING, FREEZING, DEFROSTING AND REHEATING

New to batching? This page will give you all the advice you need on how to safely store and cook food.

Refrigerating

Throughout this book you have the option to either store your meals in the fridge for a few days ahead, or in the freezer for a longer period.

- *Keep your fridge at the ideal temperature of between 3°C (37°F) and 5°C (41°F).*

- *Always store raw fish and meats on the lower shelves.*

- *Wrap food in cling film or put in food bags – it will always stay fresher and last longer if sealed.*

Freezing

The freezer is your friend when it comes to batch-cooking and getting in control of mealtimes. If you follow the meal plans in this book you will often be doubling up meals, creating one for now and one for the freezer. Understanding the basic rules of freezing food will help you become a freezing pro:

1 Label each bag with a chalk marker or a Sharpie pen. This way you won't have UFOs (unidentified frozen objects!) lurking in the freezer.

2 Ensure the meals you are batching are fully cooled before you place them in the freezer.

3 If you are freezing in a freezer bag, make sure to lay the bag flat. Once frozen you can stack them like library books, allowing you to save space and fit more in.

4 Make sure the freezer bag is completely dry on the outside before freezing, otherwise it will stick to the freezer and other bags and make it difficult to take out.

5 Don't stack multiple unfrozen bags on top of each other when putting them in the freezer – the weight will mean they all freeze together and are hard to separate.

6 Some of the recipes will ask you to prepare the meal in an ovenproof dish. I recommend using dishes that have a lid that neatly fits on top; this way it is easy to stack them in the freezer (see page 8).

If you have a small freezer, you can still batch! Even with a single freezer drawer you can get plenty of meals in there – just make sure to freeze the meals flat; then, once frozen, stack them up and you are ready to go.

TIP

When you have completed your weekly shop, it's a good idea to look at the sell-by dates to decide what may need to go in the freezer for the end of the week: fish you buy on Saturday may not last till the Friday, so either change your meal plan days around or simply freeze it until you need it.

Reheating

However you choose to reheat your frozen meal, the main point to remember is if something has been frozen and defrosted then it must be reheated until piping hot. If you are serving the meal to small children, still reheat to piping hot then allow to cool until serving temperature.

Keep forgetting to get your meals out to defrost? Set a 6pm alarm on your phone so when you're in the kitchen at dinner time the alarm will remind you to get tomorrow's meal out of the freezer.

Defrosting

Defrosting is actually very easy and simple. There are three main ways to defrost your meals.

1. IN THE FRIDGE.
Defrost frozen meals in the fridge overnight. Always put your frozen meal bag in a dish to catch any water run-off.

2. COLD WATER METHOD.
This is my favourite method as it defrosts meals fast! Place the frozen meal bag in a basin or tub of cold water (never hot!) with the seal sitting above the water line. The food will start to defrost within 20 minutes. Just ensure the cold water only touches the outside of the bag and is never in direct contact with the food.

3. DEFROST SETTING ON THE MICROWAVE.
Make sure you always remove the food from the freezer bag before you start and use a microwave-safe bowl or container. Follow the instructions on the microwave and give the food a stir halfway through the defrosting cycle.

Just remember, once raw food has been defrosted, it cannot be frozen again unless it has been cooked. Once defrosted your food should be cooked and eaten within 48 hours.

BATCHING ON A BUDGET

Series 1 and 2 of the *Batch from Scratch* TV series showed every family saving a huge amount of money each month, simply by following the changes below. It's actually very easy to reduce your food spend when you start to think, shop and cook in the Batch from Scratch way.

- Always have a plan, even if it's not for the full week. Having a rough plan of what you're going to eat will help you reduce spending and food waste.

- Once you have your plan, create a shopping list before you leave home – that way you can see what you already have and what needs to be used up.

- Once in the supermarket, stick to buying just what's on your list.

- Try to limit the amount of times you go back to the store each week; remember, the more often you go, the more you spend!

Portion Control

When making meals, try to stick to the correct portion size as indicated in the recipe. If it says serves four, then portion it out for four – it's cheaper and easier to bulk meals out with sides such as extra veg, garlic bread, etc., than to make more of the main meal.

If you're doubling up recipes and making one for the fridge and one for the freezer, make sure that the one going into the freezer is portioned out and put away to stop any overeating.

Using measuring cups (see page 9) is a great way to portion out meals: 1 cup is generally an adult portion of curry or bolognese, ½ cup is generally a small child's portion (depending on the size of the child). Portion control is often one of the main issues of overspending.

Simple Substitutes

FRUIT, VEG AND HERBS

Frozen fruits, vegetables and herbs are generally around 20 per cent cheaper than fresh, so if you are buying veg to cook with or fruit for smoothies, consider buying frozen instead of fresh. Frozen herbs are now very popular and can save you money and reduce waste, as you simply scoop out the amount you need and put the rest back in the freezer.

LENTILS AND BEANS

Consider reducing the meat in a recipe like a bolognese or chilli by half. It's such an easy tip to use 50 per cent minced meat and replace the other half with lentils. Not only will it save you money but it's healthier too. You may find that your family don't even notice as the textures are so similar.

CHEESE

INSTEAD OF	BUY
Parmesan	grana padano
feta	Greek salad cheese
branded cream cheese	supermarket own brand

These simple swaps give you the same ingredient but at a much lower cost. I guarantee you won't notice the difference except in your wallet!

FISH

INSTEAD OF	BUY
cod	coley
salmon	trout
haddock	hake

Fish that is caught on our own shores is often cheaper than imported varieties. These swaps are easy to make; again you won't really notice the difference, but it will save you money and is a lot more sustainable for the planet.

MEAT

INSTEAD OF	BUY
sirloin	brisket
flank steak	skirt steak
chicken mince	turkey mince
chicken breast fillets	chicken thighs or drumsticks
leg of lamb	lamb shank

Consider using cheaper cuts of meat as they often have just as much flavour; you simply have to cook them slightly longer to get the same softness. Simple swaps can make huge savings.

MEAL PLANNING

We all lead busy lives, rushing around trying to juggle work, kids and family life. Often how and what we eat gets affected – we try to find a quick fix, which can mean resorting to expensive takeaways and heavily processed ready meals. That's where meal planning comes in. Being organised in advance with what you are going to eat is the ultimate time- and money-saving hack. Taking just 5–10 minutes a week out of your busy life to think what you are going to eat will free up headspace and ensure you are eating delicious healthy meals without any of the stress. The meal plans in this book are based on a 28-day plan that is divided into 4 weeks, giving you the option to plan for just one week or the whole month.

The Meal Plans

In series 1 and 2 of *Batch from Scratch* the families were given a 28-day meal planner incorporating all their breakfasts, lunches and dinners. This book gives you the same. If you follow the whole 28-day plan, you may see some main dishes are repeated, so some meals you make in week 1 you will also have in week 3 but served in different ways with different sides. This means that you will have nights where you make double (I call this one for now/one for the freezer), so that at some point in the plan you can just pull out a meal from the freezer and have a night off cooking from scratch.

SHOPPING LISTS

If you are doing some doubling up nights (one for now/one for the freezer) remember you will have to add double the ingredients for that meal – simply add 'x2' next to the meals you wish to double when writing your shopping list. And if you get into double batching at the beginning of the month, you may find that you can cross off some of the meals on your shopping list later in the month, as you will have already made them.

COSTS

No exact prices have been added to this book as the price of food fluctuates so much at the moment. However, these meal plans and recipes have been designed to be very low cost, and could be even lower if you substitute some of the more expensive items, such as cod for hake or beef mince for turkey mince. If you double up any of the meals then your overall cost per meal will come down, as you will only have to buy a few extra ingredients to bulk it out – you'll have items such as the herbs and spices from the original recipe left over.

BATCHING SESSIONS

The 28-day meal plan is divided into four weeks, with each week having its own guide attached. This guide helps you plan your start of week batching and your midweek batching, so you have very little do on the other days.

Getting Started

Firstly, write down your go-to meals and any of the recipes that you like the look of in this book. Slot these into the blank planners on pages 37–40 along with your family favourite recipes.

Check your calendar and see how the coming weeks are looking: for example, which days are you out and about and which days are you quieter and could double up or make multiple dishes? Are there nights that you're cooking for fewer people or know you'll be out for dinner? Add these to the planner. If there are nights that you know are busy and will need a quick dinner before heading straight back out the door, make sure this is when you can simply reheat a freezer meal.

Once you have your plan in place, you can then create your shopping list. Write down everything you need for this week's plan, but before you leave the house cross off anything on the list that you already have in the house. That way you'll only buy exactly what's needed.

REUSING YOUR MEAL PLANS

Once you have filled in your meal plans, don't get rid of them. They are brilliant to come back to time and time again. It's work that you do once but it keeps on giving – I use my meal plans over and over again.

DESIGN YOUR OWN MEAL PLAN

By you now you will understand how these meal plans work, so use the space on pages 37–40 to fill out your own meal plans to suit you and your household. Write in pencil so that if you change your mind you can easily make any necessary adjustments.

1 28-DAY MEAL PLANNER
2 MAKING A PLAN FOR WEEK 1
3 MAKING A PLAN FOR WEEK 2
4 MAKING A PLAN FOR WEEK 3
5 MAKING A PLAN FOR WEEK 4
6 MY SHOPPING LIST

MEAL PLANNER

28-DAY MEAL PLANNER

WEEK 1

DAY	BREAKFAST	LUNCH	DINNER
Monday	Apple pie overnight oats (page 48)	Chicken mayo pittas with popcorn and fruit (page 60)	5-a-day pasta sauce with spaghetti (page 88)
Tuesday	Toast with peanut butter and banana	Tuna, sweetcorn and spring onion pasta salad (page 76)	Chicken korma with rice and naan (page 94)
Wednesday	Cereal	Chicken noodle soup jars, fruit (page 74)	Mince fajitas with wraps and salad (page 104)
Thursday	Porridge with fruit	Egg, ham and cheese muffins, popcorn (page 65)	Ratatouille-inspired hake parcels with couscous (page 110)
Friday	Yoghurt with granola and fruit	BLT pasta (page 62)	Sausage traybake (page 112)
Saturday	Fluffy pancakes with berries (page 46)	Tortilla pizzas with hummus and carrots (pages 80 and 85)	Burgers with salad and potato wedges (page 92)
Sunday	French toast with banana and maple syrup (page 47)	Baked potatoes with beans, cheese and salad (page 84)	Spatchcock Sunday chicken (page 114)

WEEK 2

DAY	BREAKFAST	LUNCH	DINNER
Monday	Porridge with banana	Chicken mayo pittas (page 60), fruit and popcorn	Katsu curry with tofu, noodles and prawn crackers (page 101)
Tuesday	Bagels with peanut butter and jam	Pesto orzo salad, hummus with carrots (pages 77 and 85)	Cheesy ham stuffed chicken breasts, potato wedges and salad (page 118)
Wednesday	Yoghurt and granola with berries	Butternut squash soup, ham sandwiches, fruit (page 71)	Mac and cheese (page 102)
Thursday	Toast and fruit	Cheese and veggie frittata, popcorn (page 67)	Slow-cooked beef massaman, rice (page 91)
Friday	Weetabix and banana	Beetroot hummus, pittas and crisps (page 85)	Chicken shawarma skewers, flatbreads and salad (page 98)
Saturday	Breakfast burritos (page 55)	Tuna melt paninis (page 61)	Homemade pizzas with salad (page 96)
Sunday	Waffles with bacon	Chicken mayo and sweetcorn pasta (page 64)	Steak pie with mashed potatoes and carrots (page 116)

WEEK 3

DAY	BREAKFAST	LUNCH	DINNER
Monday	Very berry baked oats (page 53)	Beetroot hummus and feta pittas (page 85)	5-a-day pasta sauce gnocchi bake (page 88)
Tuesday	Peanut butter and jam crumpets	Sun-dried tomato orzo pasta (page 77)	Sweet and sour chicken with noodles (page 120)
Wednesday	PBJ smoothie bags (page 49)	Tomato and basil soup, sandwiches (page 72)	Mince fajitas burrito bowls (page 104)
Thursday	Bircher muesli (page 52)	Chicken Caesar baguettes, fruit (page 60)	Sweetcorn and sage risotto (page 122)
Friday	Cereal and fruit	Greek rice salad (page 83)	Sausage traybake (page 112)
Saturday	Scrambled eggs with avocado on toast (page 49)	Ham, cheese and pesto open bagels (page 58)	Burgers in pittas with corn on the cob and coleslaw (page 92)
Sunday	Fluffy banana pancakes with yoghurt (page 46)	Baked potatoes with tuna, sweetcorn and salad (page 84)	One-tray Sunday lunch (page 109)

WEEK 4

DAY	BREAKFAST	LUNCH	DINNER
Monday	Blueberry overnight oats (page 48)	Egg, ham and cheese muffins (page 65) with salad and fruit	Katsu curry with tofu and egg fried rice (pages 101 and 68)
Tuesday	Toast with toppings and fruit	Pizza pasta salad (page 80)	Cheesy ham stuffed chicken breasts, couscous (page 118)
Wednesday	Yoghurt with granola and berries	Chunky vegetable soup, sandwiches and fruit (page 73)	Mac and cheese with crispy bacon and sweetcorn (page 102)
Thursday	Cereal	Chicken mayo pittas (page 60), fruit and popcorn	Slow-cooked beef massaman with stir-fried noodles (page 91)
Friday	Porridge with berries	Mediterranean couscous with halloumi (page 78)	Chicken shawarma skewers, rice, hummus and tomato and cucumber salad (pages 98 and 85)
Saturday	Omelette bags (page 54)	Tuna melt paninis (page 61)	Porcini mushroom alfredo bake (page 106), salad
Sunday	French toast with bacon and maple syrup (page 47)	Egg fried rice (page 68)	Beef stew with new potatoes and veg (page 116)

MAKING A PLAN FOR WEEK 1

Below are some weekly meal plans for 4 weeks, to give you some inspiration.

BREAKFASTS

MONDAY	Apple pie overnight oats (page 48)
TUESDAY	Toast with peanut butter and banana
WEDNESDAY	Cereal
THURSDAY	Porridge with fruit
FRIDAY	Yoghurt with granola and fruit
SATURDAY	Fluffy pancakes and berries (page 46)
SUNDAY	French toast with banana and maple syrup (page 47)

WHAT TO BATCH AT THE START OF THE WEEK:
Apple pie overnight oats – these will last 3 days.

WHAT TO BATCH DURING THE WEEK:
- Fluffy pancakes – while cooking your pancakes on Saturday, make double to go in the freezer for week 3.

- French toast – while cooking your French toast on Sunday, make double so you have your week 4 French toast breakfast ready and in the freezer.

TOP TIPS

- **For overnight oats** I recommend old jam jars or Kilner jars.

- **For toast**, keep your bread in the freezer and grab one slice at a time as and when you need it to avoid it going bad.

- **Leftover bananas** at the end of the week? Slice them up and freeze them to add to porridge.

- **Use frozen fruit** – it will last for as long as you need it!

MEAL PLANNER

LUNCHES

MONDAY	Chicken mayo pittas with popcorn and fruit (page 60)
TUESDAY	Tuna, sweetcorn and spring onion pasta salad (page 76)
WEDNESDAY	Chicken noodle soup jars, fruit (page 74)
THURSDAY	Egg, ham and cheese muffins, popcorn (page 65)
FRIDAY	BLT pasta (page 62)
SATURDAY	Tortilla pizzas with hummus and carrots (pages 80 and 85)
SUNDAY	Baked potatoes with beans, cheese and salad (page 84)

WHAT TO BATCH AT THE START OF THE WEEK:

- Make up your chicken mayo to fill your pittas – this will last 3 days in the fridge.

- When cooking the chicken, add an extra chicken breast to the tray and this will also do you chicken for Wednesday noodle soup jars.

- While you have the ingredients out, make up the tuna sweetcorn mayo base for the pasta salad.

WHAT TO BATCH DURING THE WEEK:

- Make your egg, ham and cheese muffins – these are a great one to double up and get in the freezer for another week.

- While these are cooking, make up the BLT pasta salad, reserving ham and cheese from the egg, ham and cheese muffins for tortilla pizzas for Saturday lunchtime.

- While making baked potatoes, cook double so you can freeze for week 3.

TOP TIPS

- Any **leftover pittas** can be frozen for another week.

- Use Kilner jars or old jam jars for the noodle soup jars.

- Any **leftover ham and grated cheese** can be added to a freezer bag and frozen ready to top tortilla pizzas another week.

DINNERS

MONDAY	5-a-day pasta sauce with spaghetti (page 88)
TUESDAY	Chicken korma with rice and naan (page 94)
WEDNESDAY	Mince fajitas with wraps and salad (page 104)
THURSDAY	Ratatouille-inspired hake parcels with couscous (page 110)
FRIDAY	Sausage traybake (page 112)
SATURDAY	Burgers with salad and potato wedges (page 92)
SUNDAY	Spatchcock Sunday chicken (page 114)

WHAT TO BATCH AT THE START OF THE WEEK:

- While the pasta sauce is cooking for Monday's 5-a-day pasta sauce, make up the mince fajita Grab and Cook bag for Wednesday.

- While the chicken korma is cooking on Tuesday night, prep the ratatouille-inspired hake parcels for Thursday. I recommend making double to take out of the freezer for another week.

- The sausage traybake is a Grab and Cook bag, so I recommend making double now and you've got your sausage traybake for week 3 in the freezer. While this is cooking, prepare your Sunday spatchcock chicken for the fridge and cover well so it is ready to go for Sunday.

- Burgers on Saturday are a great one to batch – double the recipe and you've got your burgers ready for week 3.

TOP TIPS

- Any **leftover veggies** can also be added the pasta sauce.

- **Freeze any leftover naan** for future curry nights.

- **Buy your fajita seasoning in a jar** rather than packets or make your own.

MEAL PLANNER

MAKING A PLAN FOR WEEK 2

BREAKFASTS

MONDAY	Porridge with banana
TUESDAY	Bagels with peanut butter and jam
WEDNESDAY	Yoghurt and granola with berries
THURSDAY	Toast and fruit
FRIDAY	Weetabix and banana
SATURDAY	Breakfast burritos (page 55)
SUNDAY	Waffles with bacon

WHAT TO BATCH AT THE START OF THE WEEK:
If you want to get ahead, you can make your breakfast burritos ready for the weekend. These are great to make double batches of for quick easy breakfasts. Just make sure to defrost the night before you want to eat them, then they are ready to go into the air fryer or oven.

TOP TIPS

- Any **leftover bagels and bread** can be placed in a freezer bag and frozen for another week.

- Any **leftover bananas** are great chopped and frozen to add to your smoothie bags.

LUNCHES

MONDAY	Chicken mayo pittas (page 60), fruit, popcorn
TUESDAY	Pesto orzo salad, hummus with carrots (pages 77 and 85)
WEDNESDAY	Butternut squash soup, ham sandwiches, fruit (page 71)
THURSDAY	Cheese and veggie frittata, popcorn (page 67)
FRIDAY	Beetroot hummus, pittas and crisps (page 85)
SATURDAY	Tuna melt paninis (page 61)
SUNDAY	Chicken mayo and sweetcorn pasta (page 64)

WHAT TO BATCH AT THE START OF THE WEEK:

- When making up your chicken and cream cheese wraps, why not make the ham sandwiches for Wednesday and paninis for Saturday lunches? These can all be stored in the freezer ready to grab in the morning – by lunchtime they will be defrosted.

- When making the hummus, make one batch and place into ice-cube trays to pop out and defrost for easy snacks. Make a second batch, adding the beetroot for Friday's lunch. This can easily be stored in a container or in ice-cube trays in the same way.

WHAT TO BATCH DURING THE WEEK:

- While you are making the butternut squash soup, prepare the veggie frittata.

- Use macaroni or shell pasta for the pesto pasta salad and cook double (enough for the mac and cheese) – this will save you a step on Wednesday evening.

TOP TIPS

- Any **leftover pittas** can be used instead of flatbreads with Friday's chicken shawarma skewers.

- Ensure you have a **mini Thermos** for easy take-to-work or school soup.

MEAL PLANNER

DINNERS

MONDAY	Katsu curry with tofu, noodles and prawn crackers (page 101)
TUESDAY	Cheesy ham stuffed chicken breasts, potato wedges and salad (page 118)
WEDNESDAY	Mac and cheese (page 102)
THURSDAY	Slow-cooked beef massaman, rice (page 91)
FRIDAY	Chicken shawarma skewers, flatbreads and salad (page 98)
SATURDAY	Homemade pizzas with salad (page 96)
SUNDAY	Steak pie with mashed potatoes and carrots (page 116)

WHAT TO BATCH AT THE START OF THE WEEK:
- When breading the tofu for the katsu curry, make double. It freezes great and is perfect to have in the freezer for another meal in week 4.

- Prep the stuffed chicken breasts – these are a Grab and Cook recipe, so great to make double of and fill the freezer, again saving you time in week 4.

WHAT TO BATCH DURING THE WEEK:
- When making your mac and cheese, make double the sauce and freeze flat in a small bag. The extra sauce will be great for an easy mac and cheese week in week 4. If you followed the lunch menu on page 29 you should have your pasta cooked so you just need to stir that through the sauce.

- While your mac and cheese is cooking, make up your beef massaman and chicken shawarma Grab and Cook bags. If you can make double of these they can simply be pulled out of the freezer on week 4.

TOP TIPS

- **Use packet rice**, it is super quick to heat up and works great. It is one of my favourite hacks.

- **Any leftover curry pastes or sauces** can be added to ice-cube trays and frozen ready for another week.

- Use **shop-bought mashed potatoes** from the chilled section; it's a great product and most versions don't contain any additives.

MAKING A PLAN FOR WEEK 3

BREAKFASTS

MONDAY	Very berry baked oats (page 53)
TUESDAY	Peanut butter and jam crumpets
WEDNESDAY	PBJ smoothie bags (page 49)
THURSDAY	Bircher muesli (page 52)
FRIDAY	Cereal and fruit
SATURDAY	Scrambled eggs with avocado on toast (page 49)
SUNDAY	Fluffy banana pancakes with yoghurt (page 46)

WHAT TO BATCH AT THE START OF THE WEEK:
- Very berry baked oats – these are a great one to double and freeze for another week.

- PBJ smoothie bags – these can be prepped and placed in the freezer ready to grab and add liquid for a quick morning breakfast.

WHAT TO BATCH DURING THE WEEK:
While making Saturday's scrambled eggs and avocado, prep double the amount of avocado, mash up and add to ice-cube trays and freeze ready to enjoy as a topping on toast for breakfast in week 4.

TOP TIPS

- Any **leftover crumpets** should be added to a freezer bag and frozen ready to grab when needed. These can be toasted from frozen.

- Use **frozen berries** to add to the overnight oats and in smoothies, they are cheaper and will last in the freezer for whenever you need them.

MEAL PLANNER

LUNCHES

MONDAY	Beetroot hummus and feta pittas (page 85)
TUESDAY	Sun-dried tomato orzo pasta (page 77)
WEDNESDAY	Tomato and basil soup, sandwiches (page 72)
THURSDAY	Chicken Caesar baguettes, fruit (page 60)
FRIDAY	Greek rice salad (page 83)
SATURDAY	Ham, cheese and pesto open bagels (page 58)
SUNDAY	Baked potatoes with tuna, sweetcorn and salad (page 84)

WHAT TO BATCH AT THE START OF THE WEEK:
Make up the orzo pasta salad at the start of the week – this will last 3 days in the fridge. While the pasta is cooking, get the tomato and basil soup on to cook. I recommend making double and freezing portions for another week.

WHAT TO BATCH DURING THE WEEK:
While the chicken is cooking for the chicken Caesar baguettes, cook the baked potatoes for Sunday's lunch. While these are in the oven, make up the Greek rice salad for Thursday.

TOP TIPS

- Any **leftover ham** from Tuesday's pasta salad can be kept for Saturday's ham, cheese and pesto open bagels.

- Any **lettuce** from the chicken Caesar baguettes can be chopped and stirred through the Greek rice salad.

- **Baked potatoes** freeze well, so why not cook a few while the oven is on?

DINNERS

MONDAY	5-a-day pasta sauce gnocchi bake (page 88)
TUESDAY	Sweet and sour chicken with noodles (page 120)
WEDNESDAY	Mince fajitas burrito bowls (page 104)
THURSDAY	Sweetcorn and sage risotto (page 122)
FRIDAY	Sausage traybake (page 112)
SATURDAY	Burgers in pittas with corn on the cob and coleslaw (page 92)
SUNDAY	One-tray Sunday lunch (page 109)

WHAT TO BATCH AT THE START OF THE WEEK:
If you made double of lots of the recipes in week 1, you will have very little cooking and prep to do this week as lots of your meals will come out of the freezer. If not, follow these tips.

TOP TIPS

- While the pasta sauce is cooking, make up the mince fajita Grab and Cook bag for Wednesday.

- While the sausage traybake is cooking on Friday, prepare your Sunday spatchcock chicken for the fridge and cover well so it is ready to go for Sunday.

- Any leftover veggies can also be added to the pasta sauce.

- Buy your fajita seasoning in a jar rather than packets or make your own.

MEAL PLANNER

MAKING A PLAN FOR WEEK 4

BREAKFASTS

MONDAY	Blueberry overnight oats (page 48)
TUESDAY	Toast with toppings and fruit
WEDNESDAY	Yoghurt with granola and berries
THURSDAY	Cereal
FRIDAY	Porridge with berries
SATURDAY	Omelette bags (page 54)
SUNDAY	French toast with bacon and maple syrup (page 47)

WHAT TO BATCH AT THE START OF THE WEEK:
Blueberry overnight oats – these will last for 3 days in the fridge.

WHAT TO BATCH DURING THE WEEK:
- When making omelettes, make up omelette bags with the toppings you like. These can be frozen and are then ready to use whenever you need.

- French toast is a great one to batch, double the recipe and get another batch in the freezer for another week.

TOP TIPS

- Use **Kilner jars** or old jam jars for overnight oats.

- **Sliced bread** is a great one to freeze – just grab however many slices you need and toast from frozen.

- **Frozen berries** are great to save money – they can be stored in the freezer for whenever you need.

LUNCHES

MONDAY	Egg, ham and cheese muffins (page 65) with salad and fruit
TUESDAY	Pizza pasta salad (page 80)
WEDNESDAY	Chunky vegetable soup, sandwiches and fruit (page 73)
THURSDAY	Chicken mayo pittas (page 60), fruit and popcorn
FRIDAY	Mediterranean couscous with halloumi (page 78)
SATURDAY	Tuna melt paninis (page 61)
SUNDAY	Egg fried rice (page 68)

WHAT TO BATCH AT THE START OF THE WEEK:
When making ham and cheese wraps, also make up the sandwiches to go with Wednesday's soup. These wraps and sandwiches can be frozen – no need to defrost in the morning, just add to your lunchbox frozen and they will be defrosted by lunch.

WHAT TO BATCH DURING THE WEEK:
While making the vegetable soup, make up the chicken mayo pittas for Thursday lunchtime and prep the tuna melt paninis for Saturday.

TOP TIPS

- For the **chunky vegetable soup**, make up Grab and Cook bags for another week with any leftover veg needing using in the fridge. Chop it up and store in the freezer.

- Any **leftover muffins or pittas** can be frozen for another week.

MEAL PLANNER

DINNERS

MONDAY	Katsu curry with tofu and egg fried rice (pages 101 and 68)
TUESDAY	Cheesy ham stuffed chicken breasts, couscous (page 118)
WEDNESDAY	Mac and cheese with crispy bacon and sweetcorn (page 102)
THURSDAY	Slow-cooked beef massaman with stir-fried noodles (page 91)
FRIDAY	Chicken shawarma skewers, rice, hummus and tomato and cucumber salad (pages 98 and 85)
SATURDAY	Porcini mushroom alfredo bake, salad (page 106)
SUNDAY	Beef stew with new potatoes and veg (page 116)

WHAT TO BATCH AT THE START OF THE WEEK:
If you made double of lots of the recipes in week 2, you will have very little cooking and prep to do this week as lots of your meals will come out of the freezer. If not simply follow these tips:

WHAT TO BATCH DURING THE WEEK:
- Prepare the katsu tofu and the katsu curry sauce for Monday evening.
- While the beef massaman is cooking why not prepare the chicken shawarma for the fridge?
- You could also prepare the cheese sauce for the porcini mushroom alfredo bake to make for a quick assembly when needed on Saturday.

TOP TIP

- Any **leftover hummus** freezes great for another week, just add to a container and freeze!

TIP
Write in pencil so you can use again

WEEK 1

DAY	BREAKFAST	LUNCH	DINNER
Monday			
Tuesday			
Wednesday			
Thursday			
Friday			
Saturday			
Sunday			

MEAL PLANNER

WEEK 2

DAY	BREAKFAST	LUNCH	DINNER
Monday			
Tuesday			
Wednesday			
Thursday			
Friday			
Saturday			
Sunday			

WEEK 3

DAY	BREAKFAST	LUNCH	DINNER
Monday			
Tuesday			
Wednesday			
Thursday			
Friday			
Saturday			
Sunday			

MEAL PLANNER

WEEK 4

DAY	BREAKFAST	LUNCH	DINNER
Monday			
Tuesday			
Wednesday			
Thursday			
Friday			
Saturday			
Sunday			

MY SHOPPING LIST

TIP
Write in pencil so you can use again

Write yours here

Fresh fruit, veg and herbs

Dairy

Frozen or chilled

Store cupboard

Meat and fish

Fresh fruit, veg and herbs

Write yours here

Dairy

Frozen or chilled

Store cupboard

Meat and fish

Write yours here

Fresh fruit, veg and herbs

Dairy

Frozen or chilled

Store cupboard

Meat and fish

MY SHOPPING LIST

1. FLUFFY PANCAKES
2. FRENCH TOAST
3. APPLE PIE OVERNIGHT OATS
4. SCRAMBLED EGGS WITH AVOCADO ON TOAST
5. PBJ SMOOTHIE BAGS
6. BIRCHER MUESLI
7. VERY BERRY BAKED OATS
8. OMELETTE BAGS
9. BREAKFAST BURRITOS

BREAKFASTS

FLUFFY PANCAKES

These can be made up in advance as they freeze brilliantly so you can grab them whenever you need! Great for a weekend breakfast or afternoon snack. To make banana pancakes, simply add 1 mashed banana and ½ teaspoon of ground cinnamon to the mix.

Prep: 5 minutes | **Cook:** 15 minutes | **Serves:** 4

 COOK AHEAD

 **IF MAKING AHEAD FOR THE FRIDGE OR FREEZER**

2½ cups (300g) self-raising flour

1 tsp baking powder

1 tbsp caster sugar

2 eggs

1¼ cups (300ml) milk

knob of butter

1. Add the flour, baking powder and sugar to a bowl and mix together, then create a well in the centre.
2. Add the eggs and milk to the well and whisk using a hand-held mixer until you have a lovely smooth, lump-free batter.
3. Place a non-stick frying pan over a medium heat and add the butter. Once melted, add spoonfuls of the mixture, about 2 or 3 at a time, and cook the pancakes for a couple of minutes on each side until puffed up and golden. Remove from the pan and repeat with the rest of the batter.
4. Once cooled, stack the pancakes up on top of each other with a slice of baking parchment in between each one (this will stop the pancakes from sticking to each other). Add to a freezer bag and place in the freezer.

READY TO EAT

Remove from the freezer and leave to defrost. Eat cold or, once defrosted, reheat in the toaster, microwave or in the oven for a couple of minutes. Top with whatever you fancy!

IF COOKING NOW

Follow the method for 'if making ahead' until the end of step 3.

FRENCH TOAST

The perfect weekend brunch, French toast is a brilliant recipe to make in advance for the freezer. So easy and delicious!

Prep: 5 minutes | **Cook:** 25 minutes | **Serves:** 4

V COOK AHEAD

3 eggs
splash of milk
½ tsp ground cinnamon
4 slices of bread
knob of butter

IF MAKING AHEAD FOR THE FRIDGE OR FREEZER

1. In a shallow dish, whisk the eggs, milk and cinnamon together.
2. Dip the bread slices one by one into the egg mix, making sure to coat well on both sides.
3. Place a frying pan over a medium heat and add the butter. Once melted, add a sliced of soaked bread and fry for 2–3 minutes on each side until golden.
4. Repeat with the rest of the bread.
5. Leave to cool, then add to a labelled freezer bag with a slice of baking parchment in between the slices to stop them sticking. Freeze flat.

MICROWAVE

Remove from the freezer and add a frozen slice of French toast to a plate. Microwave for 1–2 minutes until warmed through.

 IF COOKING NOW

Follow the method for 'if making ahead' until the end of step 4, then enjoy straight away with some slices of bacon, mixed berries and maple syrup for an extravagant brunch.

APPLE PIE OVERNIGHT OATS

A great make-ahead breakfast; it's not freezable, but you can make it up at the start of the week and keep in the fridge for up to 3 days. I like to use old jam jars to store individual portions, but any Tupperware will do.

Prep: 5 minutes | **Serves:** 4

V

IF MAKING AHEAD FOR THE FRIDGE

1½ cups (160g) oats

1⅓ cups (320ml) apple juice

4 heaped tbsp Greek yoghurt

2 apples, grated

ground cinnamon, to sprinkle

1. Find 4 small containers with lids and add 40g oats, ⅓ cup (80ml) apple juice and 1 heaped tablespoon of Greek yoghurt to each one. Mix well to combine.

2. Mix in the grated apple, add a sprinkle of cinnamon and mix again. Pop the lids on and keep in the fridge until needed.

TIP

To make blueberry overnight oats, substitute the grated apples for 4 handfuls of blueberries.

SCRAMBLED EGGS WITH AVOCADO ON TOAST

Scrambled eggs and avocado, a classic for a reason! My favourite dish to wake up to.

Prep: 5 minutes | **Cook:** 5 minutes | **Serves:** 4

IF COOKING NOW

8 eggs

large knob of butter

4 slices of sourdough

2 avocados, sliced

salt and pepper

1. Add the eggs and some salt and pepper to a bowl and whisk.
2. Place a frying pan over a low heat and melt the butter. Add the beaten egg and let it cook for a minute or two, then use a spatula to pull the egg into the middle of the pan as it cooks.
3. When the eggs are nearly ready, toast the sourdough. Serve the eggs on the sourdough toast with the avocado alongside.

PBJ SMOOTHIE BAGS

A fruity and nutritious way to start the day, perfect for a quick breakfast!

Prep: 5 minutes | **Makes:** enough for 4

IF MAKING AHEAD FOR THE FRIDGE OR FREEZER

1 cup (140g) frozen blueberries

1 cup (140g) frozen raspberries

2 bananas, diced into chunks

2 tbsp peanut butter

4 tbsp Greek yoghurt

2 cups (480ml) milk or water

Place everything, except the milk or water, in a large labelled freezer bag and seal. Freeze flat.

READY TO MAKE

Tip the contents of the freezer bag into a blender along with the milk or water and blend until smooth.

BREAKFASTS

Bircher muesli

Fluffy pancakes

Very berry baked oats

BIRCHER MUESLI

These prep-ahead breakfast pots are a brilliant way to start the day: very healthy and so delicious! They are not freezable but can be made in advance and kept in the fridge.

Prep: 5 minutes | **Serves:** 4

V | **GRAB AND COOK**

IF MAKING AHEAD FOR THE FRIDGE

1¾ cups (400g) Greek yoghurt

1 cup (100g) oats

4 green apples, grated

40g dried cranberries

4 tsp honey

20g pumpkin seeds

extra dried cranberries and pumpkin seeds for topping, optional

1. Find 4 small containers with lids. Add all the ingredients except those for topping to a large bowl and mix well, then distribute evenly between the 4 containers.

2. Pop the lids on and store in the fridge for up to 3 days.
3. Serve with your favourite toppings.

VERY BERRY BAKED OATS

These baked oats are a super nutritious breakfast. Cut into squares and take on the go for easy mess-free eating.

Prep: 5 minutes | **Cook:** 25–30 minutes | **Makes:** 6 slices

  COOK AHEAD

2 cups (200g) jumbo oats
1 tsp baking powder
2 cups (480ml) milk
2 tbsp honey
100g raspberries
100g blueberries
1 large banana, mashed
½ cup (45g) flaked almonds

IF MAKING AHEAD FOR THE FRIDGE OR FREEZER

1. Preheat the oven to 180°C/160°C fan and lightly grease a 20cm square tin.
2. Add all the ingredients to a large bowl and mix well. Pour into the greased tin and bake for 25–30 minutes until golden.
3. Remove from the oven and leave to cool in the tin for 15 minutes, then cut into 6 squares.
4. Once cooled, use a spatula to transfer the squares to a labelled freezer bag. Seal and freeze flat.

OVEN

Preheat the oven to 180°C/160°C fan. Remove slices of baked oats from the freezer, place on a baking tray and cover with foil. Bake for 20–25 minutes to defrost and heat through.

IF COOKING NOW

Follow the method for 'if making ahead' until the end of step 3. These are now ready to enjoy!

OMELETTE BAGS

These brilliant freezer omelette bags are fab for when you need a quick, healthy breakfast but are short on time.

Prep: 5 minutes | **Makes:** 4

GRAB AND COOK

4 slices of ham, diced

1 cup (175g) frozen peppers

12 fresh mushrooms, diced

12 cherry tomatoes, halved

1 cup (115g) frozen diced onions

To cook

oil, for frying

8 eggs

splash of milk

❄ IF MAKING AHEAD FOR THE FRIDGE OR FREEZER

1. Take 4 sealable freezer bags and fill each one with a quarter of the ingredients (do not add the oil, eggs or milk).

2. Label the bags and seal, then freeze flat.

HOB

Add a splash of oil to a large frying pan and add the frozen ingredients to the pan. Cook over a medium-high heat until everything is cooked through and piping hot (about 5 minutes). Remove from the heat. Add another splash of oil to a small omelette pan, beat 2 of the eggs mixed with a splash of milk and then pour the beaten egg into the pan. Once the base starts to cook, add the cooked filling and finish cooking your omelette. Repeat to make more omelettes.

IF COOKING NOW

Add a splash of oil to large frying pan. Add all the filling ingredients and cook over a medium-high heat until everything is cooked through and piping hot (about 5 minutes). Remove from the heat. Add another splash of oil to a small omelette pan, beat 2 of the eggs mixed with a splash of milk and then pour the beaten egg into the pan. Once the base starts to cook, add the cooked filling and finish cooking your omelette. Repeat to make more omelettes.

MAKE IT VEGGIE

Omit the ham and add any other veggies you enjoy, such as sweetcorn.

BREAKFAST BURRITOS

A delicious way to start the day, these freeze brilliantly!

Prep: 15 minutes | **Cook:** 20 minutes | **Makes:** 4

COOK AHEAD

4 pork sausages

knob of butter

8 eggs, beaten

4 large tortilla wraps

1½ cups (140g) grated Cheddar

2 handfuls fresh spinach

❄ IF MAKING AHEAD FOR THE FRIDGE OR FREEZER

1. Preheat the oven to 200°C/180°C fan. Place the sausages on a lined tray and cook for 15–20 minutes.
2. Meanwhile, add a knob of butter to a frying pan over a low-medium heat. Once melted, add the beaten eggs and cook as you would scrambled egg. Once cooked, set aside on a plate.
3. Remove the cooked sausages from the oven and slice in half lengthways.
4. Place the 4 wraps on your work surface. Distribute the scrambled egg down the centre of each wrap and top with 2 sausage halves. Distribute the grated cheese and spinach evenly between all the wraps. Roll up each wrap into a burrito.
5. Wrap each burrito tightly in tin foil, then place into a large labelled freezer bag and freeze flat.

OVEN

Remove from the freezer and leave to defrost. Preheat the oven to 180°C/160°C fan. Put the burritos on a lined tray and cook in the oven for 20 minutes until piping hot.

🍲 IF COOKING NOW

Follow the method for 'if making ahead' until the end of step 4.

OVEN

Reduce the oven temperature to 180°C/160°C fan, place the burritos on a lined tray and cook for 10 minutes, then slice up and enjoy.

Use vegetarian sausages.

BREAKFASTS

1. HAM, CHEESE AND PESTO OPEN BAGELS
2. CHICKEN CAESAR BAGUETTES
3. CHICKEN MAYO PITTAS
4. TUNA MELT PANINIS
5. BLT PASTA
6. CHICKEN MAYO AND SWEETCORN PASTA
7. EGG, HAM AND CHEESE MUFFINS
8. CHEESE AND VEGGIE FRITTATA
9. EGG FRIED RICE
10. BUTTERNUT SQUASH SOUP
11. TOMATO AND BASIL SOUP
12. CHUNKY VEGETABLE SOUP
13. CHICKEN NOODLE SOUP JARS
14. TUNA, SWEETCORN AND SPRING ONION PASTA SALAD
15. SUN-DRIED TOMATO ORZO PASTA
16. PESTO ORZO SALAD
17. MEDITERRANEAN COUSCOUS WITH HALLOUMI
18. TORTILLA PIZZAS
19. PIZZA PASTA SALAD
20. GREEK RICE SALAD
21. FREEZABLE BAKED POTATOES
22. HUMMUS

LUNCHES

HAM, CHEESE AND PESTO OPEN BAGELS

These are the perfect after-school snack or easy lunch. I make them in advance as having these pre-made and ready to grab stops me spending on takeaway lunches.

Prep: 10 minutes | **Cook:** 10 minutes | **Serves:** 4

GRAB AND COOK

- 8 tbsp pesto
- 4 bagels, halved
- 8 slices of thick ham
- 8 handfuls grated Cheddar

IF MAKING AHEAD FOR THE FRIDGE OR FREEZER

1. Spread 1 tablespoon of pesto over each half bagel and then add 1 slice of ham and a handful of grated cheese to each half.

2. Wrap each half bagel individually in cling film or foil and then place in a large labelled freezer bag and seal. Freeze flat.

OVEN

Preheat the oven to 180°C/160°C fan. Unwrap the bagel halves and place on a lined tray. Bake for 9–10 minutes until the cheese is lovely and bubbling.

IF COOKING NOW

Follow the method for 'if making ahead' until the end of step 1.

OVEN

Preheat the grill and cook the bagel halves on a baking tray for 6–8 minutes until the cheese is lovely and bubbling.

MAKE IT VEGGIE

Use plant-based ham and ensure your pesto is veggie.

LUNCHES

CHICKEN CAESAR BAGUETTES

Although not freezable this is a good one to prep in advance as the filling will keep for up to 3 days in the fridge. Then simply slice open a baguette, add the filling and go!

Prep: 5 minutes | **Makes:** 4

- 2 chicken breasts, cooked
- 3 tbsp mayonnaise
- 20g grated Parmesan
- 1 tsp Worcestershire sauce
- juice of ½ lemon
- ½ tsp garlic granules
- 4 small (individual portion) baguettes
- 1 romaine lettuce, shredded

❄ IF MAKING AHEAD FOR THE FRIDGE

Shred the cooked chicken and add to a bowl with the mayo, Parmesan, Worcestershire sauce, lemon juice and garlic granules. Mix well, then cover with cling film and transfer to the fridge.

READY TO MAKE

Slice open the baguettes and fill with the shredded lettuce and prepared chicken mixture.

CHICKEN MAYO PITTAS

My favourite sandwich filler! These are not freezable but will keep in the fridge for up to 3 days.

Prep: 5 minutes | **Makes:** 4

- 2 cooked chicken breasts, shredded
- 4 tbsp mayonnaise
- 4 pitta breads
- 1 romaine lettuce, shredded
- 10 cherry tomatoes, halved
- salt and pepper

❄ IF MAKING AHEAD FOR THE FRIDGE

1 Add the cooked chicken to a bowl with the mayonnaise. Season with salt and pepper.

2 Mix well, then cover with cling film and transfer to the fridge.

READY TO MAKE

Slice the pittas in half and open them up, then spoon the chicken mix inside, adding some shredded lettuce and cherry tomatoes to each one.

TUNA MELT PANINIS

Crispy, cheesy and packed with flavour, these tuna melt paninis are so comforting!

Prep: 5 minutes | **Cook:** 10 minutes | **Makes:** 4

2 x 145g tins of tuna, drained

1 red onion, finely diced

3 heaped tbsp mayonnaise

4 panini rolls

4 handfuls grated Cheddar

salt and pepper

❄ IF MAKING AHEAD FOR THE FRIDGE OR FREEZER

1. Mix the tuna, red onion and mayonnaise in a small bowl.
2. Split the panini rolls and spread the tuna mayonnaise evenly between them.
3. Add the grated Cheddar to each half, then top with a panini lid.
4. Wrap individually in foil, then place into a labelled freezer bag, seal and freeze flat.

 MICROWAVE & PANINI MACHINE

Remove from the freezer and unwrap. Place in the microwave for 2 minutes on the defrost setting and then cook in a panini machine for 4 minutes until piping hot.

IF COOKING NOW

Follow the method for 'if making ahead' until the end of step 3.

OVEN OR PANINI MACHINE

Preheat the oven to 180°C/160°C fan or turn on the panini machine. Place on a lined tray and bake in the oven for 10 minutes, or in the panini machine for 4 minutes.

LUNCHES

BLT PASTA

Great for a cold pasta lunch that the whole family can enjoy. Want to change it up? Simply swap the bacon for a large tin of drained tuna. This recipe is not freezable but can be made in advance and kept in the fridge for up to 2 days.

Prep: 5 minutes | **Serves:** 4

❄ IF MAKING AHEAD FOR THE FRIDGE

- 6 slices of bacon
- 350g pasta
- 6 tbsp mayonnaise
- 10 cherry tomatoes, halved
- 1 romaine lettuce, diced into small pieces
- salt and pepper

1. Cook the bacon in a frying pan until golden. Cut up into pieces.
2. Cook the pasta in salted boiling water following the instructions on the packet. Once cooked, drain.
3. Add the bacon, pasta, mayo, cherry tomatoes and lettuce to a mixing bowl. Season and mix.
4. Mix well and add to a Tupperware container. Once completely cool, seal and use within 2 days.

MAKE IT VEGGIE

Use plant-based bacon.

LUNCHES

CHICKEN MAYO AND SWEETCORN PASTA

I love a simple pasta salad that can be grabbed from the fridge for quick and easy lunches. This recipe is not freezable but can be made in advance and kept in the fridge for up to 2 days.

Prep: 15 minutes | **Cook:** 15 minutes | **Serves:** 4

❄ IF MAKING AHEAD FOR THE FRIDGE

- 2 chicken breasts
- 300g pasta
- 5 tbsp mayonnaise
- 1 x 325g tin of sweetcorn, drained
- salt and pepper

1. Preheat the oven to 180°C/160°C fan. Slice the chicken breasts into strips and arrange on a lined tray. Cook in the oven for 15 minutes, or until cooked through. Allow to cool, then cut into small chunks.
2. While the chicken is cooking, cook the pasta in salted boiling water following the instructions on the packet. Once cooked, drain.
3. Add the chicken and drained pasta to a bowl, then add the mayonnaise and sweetcorn. Season to taste.
4. Mix well and add to a Tupperware container. Once completely cool, seal and use within 2 days.

Swap the chicken for roasted red pepper.

EGG, HAM AND CHEESE MUFFINS

I like to think of these as little omelette cups, so simple and quick to make.

Prep: 5 minutes | **Cook:** 15–20 minutes | **Makes:** 12

COOK AHEAD

6 eggs

splash of milk

oil, for greasing

6 slices of ham, cut into small strips

⅓ cup (80g) grated Cheddar

salt and pepper

 IF MAKING AHEAD FOR THE FRIDGE OR FREEZER

1. Preheat the oven to 180°C/160°C fan.
2. Add the eggs and the splash of milk to a mixing jug and season with salt and pepper. Using a fork, give it a good whisk.
3. Grease the holes of a 12-hole muffin tin with a little oil, then distribute the ham slices between the oiled muffin holes.
4. Pour the egg mix evenly between the muffin holes and then top each with a little grated Cheddar.
5. Bake the muffins in the oven for 15–20 minutes, or until the egg mix is set.
6. Remove from the oven and leave to cool, then place into a labelled freezer bag, seal and freeze flat.

 MICROWAVE

Remove from the freezer in the morning; they will have defrosted by lunchtime so all you will need to do is reheat in the microwave for 30 seconds.

 IF COOKING NOW

Follow the method for 'if making ahead' until the end of step 5.

CHEESE AND VEGGIE FRITTATA

This prep-ahead frittata is such a winner for a quick lunch. Nutritious and delicious!

Prep: 5 minutes | **Cook:** 30 minutes | **Serves:** 4–6

 V COOK AHEAD

❄ IF MAKING AHEAD FOR THE FRIDGE OR FREEZER

oil, for frying

2 peppers, finely diced

2 large handfuls frozen peas

8 eggs

⅓ cup (80ml) milk

1½ cups (140g) grated Cheddar

salt and pepper

1. Line a 20cm square baking dish with greaseproof paper.
2. Add a splash of oil to a large frying pan and place over a medium heat. Add the diced peppers and peas cook for 5–6 minutes until soft.
3. Put the eggs and milk into a mixing jug along with a good grind of salt and pepper and whisk well.
4. Once the veggies are soft, scatter them into the baking dish, then pour over the egg mix. Scatter over the cheese and place in the oven for 20–25 minutes until the frittata is firm.
5. Once cooked, remove from the oven and leave to cool. Once cooled, slice into 4 wedges.
6. Place into a labelled freezer bag, seal and freeze flat.

MICROWAVE

Place a frozen slice of frittata in the microwave and cook for 2 minutes, or until defrosted and piping hot.

IF COOKING NOW

Follow the method for 'if making ahead' until the end of step 4. Slice and enjoy.

EGG FRIED RICE

The perfect easy lunch, and one the whole family will love! Budget-friendly and filling, this recipe is not freezable but you can make it in advance and keep it in the fridge for up to 3 days.

Prep: 5 minutes | **Cook:** 3–4 minutes | **Serves:** 4

❄ IF MAKING AHEAD FOR THE FRIDGE

1 tbsp vegetable oil

3 eggs

300g cooked rice

1 cup (140g) frozen peas

200g frozen stir-fry veggies

3 tbsp soy sauce

2 spring onions, finely sliced

1. Heat the vegetable oil in a large frying pan or wok placed over a high heat. Crack in the eggs and scramble up with a spatula; once cooked, stir through the cooked rice, peas and stir-fry vegetables. Place the lid on and cook for 3–4 minutes until the veggies are soft.
2. Add the soy sauce, stir through the spring onions and serve up.

LUNCHES

LUNCHES

BUTTERNUT SQUASH SOUP

Warming, comforting and perfect for dunking a chunk of crusty bread into.

Prep: 5 minutes | **Cook:** 30 minutes | **Serves:** 4

 VE   COOK AHEAD

❄ IF MAKING AHEAD FOR THE FRIDGE OR FREEZER

- 1 tbsp olive oil
- 1 red onion, thinly sliced
- 500g frozen butternut squash chunks
- 2 tsp frozen chopped garlic (or fresh)
- ½ tsp chilli flakes (optional)
- 3 cups (720ml) vegetable stock
- salt and pepper

1. Heat the oil in a large saucepan over a medium heat and add the onion and frozen squash chunks.
2. Cook for 2 minutes, then add the garlic, chilli (if using) and stock. Bring to the boil, then reduce to a simmer and cook for 25 minutes.
3. Once cooked, blend, then season with salt and pepper.
4. Leave to cool, then add to a large labelled freezer bag (or portion into smaller bags) and seal. Freeze flat.

 HOB

Remove the soup from the freezer and add the contents of the bag to a saucepan. Place over a low heat, breaking up the soup as it defrosts. Cook until piping hot.

 IF COOKING NOW

Follow the method for 'if making ahead' until the end of step 3.

TOMATO AND BASIL SOUP

You can't beat a classic tomato soup!

Prep: 5 minutes | **Cook:** 20 minutes | **Serves:** 4

 V   COOK AHEAD

IF MAKING AHEAD FOR THE FRIDGE OR FREEZER

1 tbsp olive oil

1 cup (115g) frozen diced onions

1 tsp garlic purée

2 x 400g tins of chopped tomatoes

3 cups (720ml) vegetable stock

large handful fresh basil

1 tbsp double cream

salt and pepper

1. Heat the olive oil in a large saucepan over a medium heat and add the onions, garlic and chopped tomatoes. Bring to the boil, then add the vegetable stock.
2. Cook for 15 minutes before adding the basil, double cream and some salt and pepper.
3. Blend the soup with a hand-held blender.
4. Leave to cool, then add to a large labelled freezer bag (or portion into smaller bags) and seal. Freeze flat.

HOB

Remove the soup from the freezer and add to a saucepan. Place over a low heat, breaking up the soup as it defrosts. Cook until piping hot.

IF COOKING NOW

Follow the method for 'if making ahead' until the end of step 3.

MAKE IT VEGAN

Use plant-based cream.

CHUNKY VEGETABLE SOUP

Hearty, wholesome and loaded with vegetables. The perfect way to warm you up on a chilly day.

Prep: 5 minutes | **Cook:** 30 minutes | **Serves:** 4

 VE COOK AHEAD

1 cup (115g) frozen diced onions

1 tsp garlic purée

2 medium carrots, peeled and finely diced

1 large courgette, finely diced

2 celery sticks, finely diced

1 tbsp tomato purée

1 tsp dried rosemary

1 vegetable stock cube, crumbled

4 cups (1 litre) boiling water

salt and pepper

❄ IF MAKING AHEAD FOR THE FRIDGE OR FREEZER

1 Add all the ingredients to a large saucepan. Bring to the boil, then reduce the heat to a simmer and cook for 25 minutes, or until the veggies are tender. Season to taste with salt and pepper.

2 Leave to cool, then add to a large labelled freezer bag (or portion into smaller bags) and seal. Freeze flat.

HOB

Remove the soup from the freezer and add to a saucepan. Place over a low heat, breaking up the soup as it defrosts. Cook until piping hot.

IF COOKING NOW

Follow the method for 'if making ahead' until the end of step 1.

CHICKEN NOODLE SOUP JARS

These are great to prep ahead for a quick take-to-work lunch. These are not freezable but can be made in advance and stored in the fridge for up to 3 days.

Prep: 10 minutes | **Makes:** 4 jars

2 nests of vermicelli noodles

80g chopped mushrooms

200g drained sweetcorn

1 head of pak choi, trimmed and sliced

handful fresh coriander

200g cooked chicken, shredded

4 tbsp soy sauce

2 chicken stock cubes

❄ IF MAKING AHEAD FOR THE FRIDGE

1. Take 4 jars and add ½ nest of noodles to each one.
2. Distribute the chopped mushrooms, sweetcorn, pak choi, coriander and cooked chicken between the 4 jars. Add 1 tablespoon of soy sauce to each one.
3. Grate ½ chicken stock cube into each jar, then pop into the fridge.

READY TO MAKE

When needed, pour over boiling water and leave to sit for 5 minutes before stirring everything together. Enjoy!

LUNCHES

TUNA, SWEETCORN AND SPRING ONION PASTA SALAD

My family's favourite on-the-go lunch – creamy tuna, crunchy sweetcorn and al dente pasta. This recipe is not freezable but can be made in advance and kept in the fridge for up to 2 days.

Prep: 12 minutes | **Serves:** 4

❄ IF MAKING AHEAD FOR THE FRIDGE

350g pasta, such as fusilli

2 x 110g tins of tuna, drained

1 x 200g tin of sweetcorn, drained

8 spring onions, finely chopped

12 cherry tomatoes, halved

4 heaped tbsp mayonnaise

salt and pepper

1. Cook the pasta following the instructions on the packet, then drain and leave to cool.
2. Add the drained tuna, drained sweetcorn, chopped spring onions, cherry tomatoes and mayonnaise to a large bowl. Season well with salt and pepper and then add the cooked pasta.
3. Transfer to a Tupperware container, cover and store in the fridge for up to 2 days.

TIP

For a hot on-the-go lunch, consider buying a good food flask and having the pasta hot. There are endless variations – change up the pasta for rice or any other flavour combinations.

SUN-DRIED TOMATO ORZO PASTA

This recipe is not freezable but will last 2–3 days in the fridge: simply stir through a splash of olive oil if slightly dry.

Prep: 12 minutes | **Serves:** 4

❄ IF MAKING AHEAD FOR THE FRIDGE

- 350g orzo pasta
- 1 x 190g jar of red pesto sauce
- 4 slices of ham, cut into chunks
- 8 sun-dried tomatoes, roughly chopped

1. Cook the pasta following the instructions on the packet, then drain and add to a large bowl. Add the pesto to the pasta along with the ham and sun-dried tomatoes and mix together.

2. Transfer to a container and allow to cool before sealing and putting in the fridge.

PESTO ORZO SALAD

A super-quick meal that is brilliant for lunchboxes. Try a jar of red pesto if you fancy a change for another week. This recipe is not freezable but will last 2–3 days in the fridge: simply stir through a splash of olive oil if slightly dry.

Prep: 12 minutes | **Serves:** 4

❄ IF MAKING AHEAD FOR THE FRIDGE

- 350g orzo pasta
- 1 x 190g jar of green pesto sauce
- 2 red peppers, diced into chunks

1. Cook the pasta following the instructions on the packet, then drain and add to a large bowl. Add the pesto to the pasta and mix.

2. Add to a container and allow to cool before mixing in the diced red pepper, sealing it and putting it in the fridge.

MEDITERRANEAN COUSCOUS WITH HALLOUMI

A fresh and delicious salad. This recipe is not freezable but can be made in advance and kept in the fridge for up to 3 days.

Prep: 15 minutes | **Serves:** 4

❄ IF MAKING AHEAD FOR THE FRIDGE

- 2 x 110g packets of dried Mediterranean-style couscous
- ½ cucumber, diced
- 10 cherry tomatoes, halved
- 1 x 400 tin of chickpeas, drained
- handful fresh parsley, finely chopped
- 3 tbsp olive oil
- juice of 1 lemon
- 1 x 225g block of halloumi, diced into chunks
- salt and pepper

1. Soak the couscous as per the packet instructions, then add the cucumber, cherry tomatoes, chickpeas and parsley. Add 2 tablespoons of the olive oil and the lemon juice and stir to combine, then season with salt and pepper.

2. Heat the remaining tablespoon of oil in a frying pan and fry the halloumi chunks over a medium heat until browned all over. Allow to cool slightly, then stir through the salad.

3. Transfer to a container and leave to cool before storing in the fridge for up to 3 days.

LUNCHES

TORTILLA PIZZAS

The perfect lunch in a hurry! Note that these are not freezable.

Prep: 15 minutes | **Makes:** 4

4 tortilla wraps

8 tbsp pizza sauce

3 cups (280g) grated Cheddar

any toppings you like: sliced peppers, mushrooms, sweetcorn or pepperoni for a meat version.

❄ IF MAKING AHEAD FOR THE FRIDGE

1. Preheat the oven to 180°C/160°C fan.
2. Lay out your wraps and spread 2 tablespoons of the tomato sauce onto each one. Distribute the cheese between the 4 wraps and then top with whatever you fancy! Slide onto baking trays.
3. Cook for 8–10 minutes, or until melted and lovely!

PIZZA PASTA SALAD

All your favourite pizza flavours in a pasta salad! This recipe is not freezable but can be made in advance and kept in the fridge for up to 2 days.

Prep: 15 minutes | **Serves:** 4

❄ IF MAKING AHEAD FOR THE FRIDGE

350g pasta

10 cherry tomatoes, halved

8 slices salami, chopped

1 x 200g tin of sweetcorn, drained

3 tbsp olive oil

1 tsp dried oregano

1 ball of mozzarella, torn

10 fresh basil leaves, lightly torn

1. Cook the pasta in salted boiling water following the instructions on the packet, then drain.
2. Add the drained pasta to a large bowl with the rest of the ingredients and toss well.
3. Add to a Tupperware container; once completely cool, seal and store in the fridge. Use within 2 days.

MAKE IT VEGGIE

Use plant-based salami.

LUNCHES

LUNCHES

GREEK RICE SALAD

A lovely healthy lunch recipe! This recipe is not freezable but can be made in advance and kept in the fridge for up to 3 days.

Prep: 5 minutes | **Serves:** 4

- 2 x pouches of ready-cooked brown rice
- 12 mixed olives, halved
- 10 cherry tomatoes, halved
- ½ cucumber, diced
- 1 romaine lettuce, roughly chopped
- 3 tbsp olive oil
- juice of 1 lemon
- 100g feta cheese, crumbled

IF MAKING AHEAD FOR THE FRIDGE

1. Combine all the ingredients in a large bowl. Toss together and store in the fridge for up to 3 days.

TIPS

I keep my rice salad in an airtight bag to stop it from drying out – the top tip for keeping food fresh is to keep it as airtight as possible.

If your rice or pasta salad is a little dry, you can add a splash of olive oil, pesto or some mayonnaise to spruce it up.

I tend to make these salads at the start of the week and then again in the middle of the week so they stay fresh.

MAKE IT VEGAN

Omit the feta or add a plant-based cheese.

FREEZABLE BAKED POTATOES

Baked potatoes can take a while to cook so I like to bake lots at the start of the week and keep them in the fridge and freezer for easy lunches.

Prep: 30 minutes | **Serves:** 4

 VE COOK AHEAD

 IF MAKING AHEAD FOR THE FRIDGE OR FREEZER

4 baking potatoes
1 tbsp olive oil
salt and pepper

1. Pierce the potatoes all over with a fork, then microwave on high for 12 minutes.
2. Preheat the oven to 200°C/180°C fan or an air fryer to 180°C.
3. Rub the microwaved potatoes with olive oil and salt and pepper. Place into the oven or air fryer and cook for 15 minutes until crisp.
4. Once cooked, leave to cool and then add to a labelled freezer bag. Transfer to the fridge or freezer.

OVEN

Remove from the freezer and leave to defrost. Reheat for 10 minutes in an oven preheated to 200°C/180°C fan.

MICROWAVE

Remove from the freezer and leave to defrost. Reheat for 2 minutes in the microwave.

IF COOKING NOW

Follow the method for 'if making ahead' until the end of step 3.

HUMMUS

The ultimate dip for a picky lunch, I adore hummus and this recipe is so simple. To make beetroot hummus, add 3 roughly chopped cooked beetroots to the blender.

Prep: 5 minutes | **Serves:** 4

1 x 400g tin of chickpeas (keep some of the liquid)

2 tbsp tahini

juice of 1 lemon

½ tsp garlic purée

1 tbsp olive oil

salt and pepper

IF MAKING AHEAD FOR THE FRIDGE OR FREEZER

1 Add everything to a blender along with ½ cup (120ml) of the chickpea liquid. Blend until smooth.

2 Add to a container or an ice-cube tray and freeze.

READY TO EAT

Remove from the freezer and leave to fully defrost. This is best done in the fridge overnight.

IF MAKING NOW

Follow the method for 'if making ahead' until the end of step 1.

1. 5-A-DAY PASTA SAUCE
2. SLOW-COOKED BEEF MASSAMAN
3. BURGERS
4. CHICKEN KORMA
5. HOMEMADE PIZZA AND CALZONES
6. CHICKEN SHAWARMA SKEWERS
7. KATSU CURRY WITH TOFU
8. MAC AND CHEESE
9. MINCE FAJITAS
10. PORCINI MUSHROOM ALFREDO BAKE
11. ONE-TRAY SUNDAY LUNCH
12. RATATOUILLE-INSPIRED HAKE PARCELS
13. SAUSAGE TRAYBAKE
14. SPATCHCOCK SUNDAY CHICKEN
15. STEAK PIE
16. CHEESY HAM STUFFED CHICKEN BREASTS
17. SWEET AND SOUR CHICKEN
18. SWEETCORN AND SAGE RISOTTO

DINNERS

5-A-DAY PASTA SAUCE

A perfect pasta sauce, full of flavour and full of veggies.

Prep: 5 minutes | **Cook:** 25–30 minutes | **Serves:** 4

 VE — COOK AHEAD

❄ IF MAKING AHEAD FOR THE FRIDGE OR FREEZER

Ingredients

- 1 tbsp olive oil
- 1 cup (115g) frozen diced onions
- 2 large carrots, peeled and finely diced
- 2 celery sticks, finely diced
- 1 courgette, finely diced
- 1 tsp garlic purée
- 2 x 400g tins of chopped tomatoes
- ½ cup (120ml) vegetable stock
- large handful fresh basil
- salt and pepper

Method

1. Add the oil to a large saucepan set over a medium heat. Add the diced onion, carrots, celery and courgette and cook for 5 minutes.
2. Stir through the garlic purée, tins of chopped tomatoes and vegetable stock.
3. Bring to the boil, then reduce to a simmer and cook for 20–25 minutes until the veggies are soft.
4. Add to a blender along with the basil leaves and blend until smooth. Season to taste.
5. Leave to cool, then add to a labelled freezer bag, seal and freeze flat.

HOB

Remove from the freezer and leave to fully defrost, then pour into a saucepan and heat through until piping hot.

MICROWAVE

Remove from the freezer and leave to fully defrost. Pour into a microwave-safe container and reheat for 2–3 minutes until piping hot.

IF COOKING NOW

Follow the method for 'if making ahead' until the end of step 4.

TIP

To make a gnocchi bake, stir a packet of gnocchi into the sauce, pour into an ovenproof dish and tear over 2 balls of mozzarella. Cook at 180°C/160°C fan for 30 minutes until golden and bubbling.

DINNERS

DINNERS

SLOW-COOKED BEEF MASSAMAN

This slow-cooked curry is so comforting. Creamy coconut, tender beef, warming spices and packed with veggies, what's not to love?

Prep: 10 minutes | **Cook:** 2–3 hours in oven, 4–7 hours in slow cooker | **Serves:** 4

GRAB AND COOK

- 750g diced stewing beef
- 1 cup (115g) frozen diced onions
- 1 tsp ginger purée
- 1 tsp garlic purée
- 2 cups (350g) frozen sliced peppers
- 2 medium sweet potatoes, scrubbed and diced into small chunks
- 2 heaped tbsp massaman curry paste
- 1 x 400ml tin of coconut milk
- 1 beef stock cube, crumbled

To cook
- 2 tbsp vegetable oil, for frying

MAKE IT VEGGIE

Use diced aubergine instead of beef and a vegetable stock cube. Reduce the cooking time to 3–4 hours on high.

❄ IF MAKING AHEAD FOR THE FRIDGE OR FREEZER

1. Add the beef to a large labelled freezer bag, and the remaining ingredients to a smaller freezer bag. Slot the smaller bag inside the larger one, then seal and freeze flat.

SLOW COOKER

Remove from the freezer and leave to fully defrost. Heat the oil in a large frying pan and brown the beef, working in batches. Transfer to the slow cooker along with the rest of the ingredients and mix well. Pop the lid on and cook for 3–4 hours on high, or 6–7 hours on low until the beef is tender. Add a splash of water if the sauce is a little thick.

OVEN

Remove from the freezer and leave to fully defrost. Preheat the oven to 160°C/140°C fan. Add the oil to a large casserole dish and brown the beef, working in batches. Add the rest of the ingredients, mix well and bring to the boil, then pop the lid on and cook in the oven for 2–3 hours until the beef is lovely and tender.

IF COOKING NOW

SLOW COOKER

Heat the oil in a large frying pan and brown the beef, working in batches. Transfer to the slow cooker along with the rest of the ingredients and mix well. Pop the lid on and cook for 3–4 hours on high, or 6–7 hours on low until the beef is tender. Add a splash of water if the sauce is a little thick. Serve with rice and enjoy!

OVEN

Preheat the oven to 160°C/140°C fan. Add the oil to a large casserole dish and brown the beef all over, working in batches. Add the rest of the ingredients, mix well and bring to the boil, then pop the lid on and cook in the oven for 2–3 hours until the beef is lovely and tender. Serve with rice and enjoy!

BURGERS

Serve in buns with salad and your favourite condiments and potato wedges on the side. Or why not cook and chop up over a salad or stuff into pittas?

Prep: 5 minutes | **Cook:** 20–25 minutes | **Serves:** 4

GRAB AND COOK

500g beef mince (10% fat)

½ beaten egg

1 tbsp American mustard

salt and pepper

To cook

oil, for frying

To serve

brioche buns

Little Gem lettuce leaves

sliced tomatoes

sliced red onion

slices of Cheddar

IF MAKING AHEAD FOR THE FRIDGE OR FREEZER

1. Add all of the ingredients to a large bowl. Using your hands, mix until everything comes together.
2. Tip out onto a work surface and divide into 4 equal portions. Roll each piece into a burger shape.
3. Place the burgers in a large labelled freezer bag with a sheet of baking parchment between each one. Freeze flat.

HOB

Remove from the freezer and leave to fully defrost. Place a frying pan over a medium heat. Add a splash of oil, then fry the burgers for 3–4 minutes on each side until cooked through.

OVEN

Remove from the freezer and leave to fully defrost. Preheat the oven to 200°C/180°C fan. Place the burgers on a tray and cook for 20–25 minutes until cooked through.

IF COOKING NOW

Follow the method for 'if making ahead' to until the end of step 2.

HOB

Place a frying pan over a medium heat. Add a splash of oil, then fry the burgers for 3–4 minutes on each side until cooked through.

OVEN

Preheat the oven to 200°C/180°C fan. Place the burgers on a tray and cook for 20–25 minutes until cooked through.

Slice open the buns, add some lettuce, tomatoes and onions, then place a burger on top of each one with a slice of cheese. Pop the lids on and enjoy.

MAKE IT VEGGIE

Use plant-based mince.

DINNERS

CHICKEN KORMA

Chicken korma is one of those dishes that I always come back to. It's a family favourite for a reason and this recipe is so simple and delicious.

Prep: 10 minutes | **Cook:** 30 minutes | **Serves:** 4

COOK AHEAD

- 1 tbsp olive oil
- 1 cup (115g) frozen diced onions
- 2 garlic cloves, crushed
- 2.5cm knob of ginger, peeled and grated
- 1 tsp ground turmeric
- 2 tsp curry powder
- 2 skinless chicken breasts, cut into small chunks
- 450g sweet potato, peeled and cut into small chunks
- 2 cups (250g) frozen mixed veg
- 1½ cups (350ml) chicken stock
- ¾ cup (200g) Greek yoghurt
- 1 tbsp mango chutney
- salt and pepper

❄ IF MAKING AHEAD FOR THE FRIDGE OR FREEZER

1. Heat the oil in a large saucepan over a medium heat. Add the diced onions, garlic and ginger. Cook for 5 minutes before adding all of the spices.
2. Cook for 1 minute, then stir through the chicken, sweet potato and frozen mixed veg. Coat well in the spices, then add the chicken stock.
3. Season with salt and pepper and bring to the boil, then reduce to a simmer and cook for 20–25 minutes.
4. Just before the end of the cooking time, stir through the Greek yoghurt and mango chutney.
5. Leave to cool, then add to a large labelled freezer bag, seal and freeze flat.

HOB

Remove from the freezer and leave to fully defrost. Once defrosted, pour into a saucepan and heat through until piping hot.

 MICROWAVE

Remove from the freezer and leave to fully defrost. Pour into a microwave-safe dish and reheat for 3–4 minutes until piping hot.

 IF COOKING NOW

Follow the method for 'if making ahead' until the end of step 4.

MAKE IT VEGGIE

Replace the chicken with a tin of drained chickpeas and use vegetable stock instead of chicken stock.

HOMEMADE PIZZA AND CALZONES

Who doesn't love a Friday pizza night? These are so simple to prep in advance!

Prep: 5 minutes | **Cook:** 15–20 minutes | **Serves:** 4

GRAB AND COOK

4 shop-bought pizza dough balls

Toppings
sliced peppers
sweetcorn
sliced mushrooms
sliced cooked chicken
2 cups (280g) grated mozzarella

In the cupboard
8 tbsp tomato passata

❄ IF MAKING AHEAD FOR THE FRIDGE OR FREEZER

1. Add your toppings of choice to a freezer bag, with the mozzarella in a smaller bag slotted inside. Freeze flat alongside your pizza dough.

🔲 OVEN

Remove the bag of toppings and pizza dough from the freezer and leave to defrost. Preheat the oven to 200°C/180°C fan. Roll out the dough balls on a work surface and top your pizzas with passata, toppings and mozzarella. If making a calzone, add the passata and toppings to one side of the dough, then fold over the top and seal the edges. Cook for 15–20 minutes until golden and bubbling.

AIR FRYER

Remove the bag of toppings and pizza dough from the freezer and leave to defrost. Preheat the air fryer to 200°C. Roll out the dough balls on a work surface and top your pizzas with passata, toppings and mozzarella. If making a calzone, add the passata and toppings to one side of the dough, then fold over the top and seal the edges. Cook for 15 minutes until golden and bubbling.

IF COOKING NOW

OVEN

Preheat the oven to 200°C/180°C fan. Roll out the dough balls on a work surface and top your pizzas with passata, toppings and mozzarella. If making a calzone, add the passata and toppings to one side of the dough, then fold over the top and seal the edges. Cook for 15–20 minutes until golden and bubbling.

AIR FRYER

Preheat the air fryer to 200°C. Roll out the dough balls on a work surface and top your pizzas with passata, toppings and mozzarella. If making a calzone, add the passata and toppings to one side of the dough, then fold over the top and seal the edges. Cook for 15 minutes until golden and bubbling.

DINNERS

CHICKEN SHAWARMA SKEWERS

These skewers are the perfect easy dinner! I like to serve with flatbreads, salad and some tzatziki.

Prep: 5 minutes | **Cook:** 10 minutes | **Serves:** 4

GRAB AND COOK

2 tsp garlic purée

1 tbsp ground coriander

1 tsp ground cumin

2 tsp smoked paprika

juice of 1 lemon

4 tbsp olive oil

1 tsp salt

8 skinless and boneless chicken thighs, cut into chunks

❄️ IF MAKING AHEAD FOR THE FRIDGE OR FREEZER

1. Combine the garlic, coriander, cumin, smoked paprika, lemon juice, olive oil and salt in a large bowl and mix into a paste.
2. Add the chicken thighs and give it a good mix.
3. Add to a labelled freezer bag, seal and freeze flat.

OVEN

Remove from the freezer and leave to fully defrost. Preheat the grill, thread the chicken onto 4 skewers and cook for 6–7 minutes on each side until the chicken is cooked through.

AIR FRYER

Remove from the freezer and leave to fully defrost. Preheat the air fryer to 200°C and thread the chicken onto 4 skewers. Cook for 10–12 minutes, turning halfway through, until the chicken is cooked through.

IF COOKING NOW

Follow the method for 'if making ahead' until the end of step 2.

OVEN

Preheat the grill, thread the chicken onto 4 skewers and cook for 6–7 minutes on each side until the chicken is cooked through.

AIR FRYER

Preheat the air fryer to 200°C and thread the chicken onto 4 skewers. Cook for 10–12 minutes, turning halfway through, until the chicken is cooked through.

DINNERS

DINNERS

100

KATSU CURRY WITH TOFU

A delicious and easy midweek veggie meal.

Prep: 5 minutes | **Cook:** 20 minutes | **Serves:** 4

 VE   COOK AHEAD

For the katsu sauce
1 tbsp vegetable oil

1 large carrot, peeled and chopped

1 cup (115g) frozen chopped onions

1 tsp garlic purée

1 tsp ginger purée

1 tbsp mild curry powder

1 tbsp agave syrup

1 tbsp soy sauce

2½ cups (600ml) vegetable stock

For the breaded tofu
600g firm tofu, cut into chunks

4 tbsp cornflour

6 tbsp water

1½ cups (68g) breadcrumbs

salt and pepper

To cook
oil, for frying

IF MAKING AHEAD FOR THE FRIDGE OR FREEZER

1. To make the sauce, heat the oil in a saucepan, add the carrot and onions and cook until softened, then add all the remaining ingredients, mix well and bring to the boil. Cook for 15 minutes until the veggies are soft, then blend until smooth.
2. Leave to cool, then add to a labelled freezer bag, seal and freeze flat.
3. To prepare the tofu, first press it with kitchen paper to remove excess moisture, then mix the cornflour and water to a paste in a shallow bowl. Add the breadcrumbs to a second bowl and season with salt and pepper.
4. Add the tofu chunks into the cornflour mix, then roll in the breadcrumbs, coating well.
5. Add to a large labelled freezer bag, seal and freeze flat.

OVEN
Preheat the oven to 200°C/180°C fan. Tip the frozen tofu onto a baking tray, drizzle with oil, then bake in the oven for 20–25 minutes until golden. Add the frozen sauce to a saucepan and heat through until piping hot.

AIR FRYER
Preheat the air fryer to 200°C. Cook the frozen tofu for 18–20 minutes, turning halfway. Break up the frozen sauce inside the bag, then add to a saucepan and heat through until piping hot.

IF COOKING NOW

Follow steps 1, 3 and 4 of the method for 'if making ahead'.

OVEN
Preheat the oven to 200°C/180°C fan. Tip the tofu onto a baking tray, drizzle with oil, then cook for 15–20 minutes until golden. Reheat the sauce in a saucepan until piping hot.

AIR FRYER
Preheat the air fryer to 200°C. Cook for 15–18 minutes, turning halfway. Reheat the sauce in a saucepan until piping hot.

MAC AND CHEESE

A good mac and cheese is something everyone needs to have up their sleeve.

Prep: 15 minutes | **Cook:** 1 hour | **Serves:** 4

 V   COOK AHEAD

IF MAKING AHEAD FOR THE FRIDGE OR FREEZER

200g pasta shapes (macaroni or shells)

50g butter

½ cup (50g) plain flour

2 cups (500ml) semi-skimmed milk

2 cups (200g) grated Cheddar

1 tsp English mustard

200g cherry tomatoes, halved

1 x 198g tin of sweetcorn, drained

½ cup (22g) breadcrumbs

salt and pepper

1. Cook the pasta in a saucepan of boiling water with a little salt for 1 minute less than the packet instructions, then drain and set aside.
2. Melt the butter in a saucepan over a medium heat, then stir through the flour and cook for a couple of minutes, stirring regularly.
3. Gradually add the milk, whisking the whole time as it thickens to a lovely thick sauce. Reduce the heat and stir through two thirds of the grated Cheddar and the mustard. Season with salt and pepper and remove from the heat.
4. Stir through the drained pasta, half the cherry tomatoes and the sweetcorn, then pour into a 2.6-litre ovenproof dish.
5. Scatter over the rest of the Cheddar, the rest of the cherry tomatoes and the breadcrumbs.
6. Pop a lid on and place into the freezer.

OVEN

Preheat the oven to 190°C/170°C fan. Remove from the freezer, remove the lid then wrap up in foil. Cook for 1 hour–1 hour 10 minutes, removing the foil after 30 minutes.

AIR FRYER

Remove from the freezer and leave to defrost. Once defrosted, preheat the air fryer to 190°C and cook for 30–40 minutes until golden and bubbling.

IF COOKING NOW

Follow the method for 'if making ahead' until the end of step 5.

OVEN

Preheat the oven to 190°C/170°C fan and cook for 35–40 minutes.

AIR FRYER

Preheat the air fryer to 190°C and cook for 20–25 minutes.

DINNERS

MINCE FAJITAS

Zhuzh these up with fresh chilli, coriander, guacamole and lots of hot sauce for the adults! Serve in wraps, or with rice, guacamole and sour cream for a burrito bowl, or why not load up into baked potatoes?

Prep: 5 minutes | **Cook:** 5–10 minutes | **Serves:** 4

COOK AHEAD

1 tbsp olive oil

500g beef mince

2 cups (350g) frozen sliced peppers

1 cup (115g) frozen diced onions

1 packet of fajita seasoning

❄ IF MAKING AHEAD FOR THE FRIDGE OR FREEZER

1. Heat the oil in a frying pan over a medium heat. Add the mince and brown all over before adding the sliced peppers and onions.
2. Cook until the peppers are soft, then add the fajita seasoning and a splash of water.
3. Once cooked, leave to cool, then add to a labelled freezer bag, seal and freeze flat.

HOB

Remove from the freezer and leave to fully defrost. Once defrosted, pour into a saucepan and heat through until piping hot. Add a splash of water if needed.

MICROWAVE

Remove from the freezer and leave to fully defrost. Pour into a microwave-safe container and reheat for 3–4 minutes until piping hot. Add a splash of water if needed.

🍲 IF COOKING NOW

Follow the method for 'if making ahead' to until the end of step 2.

MAKE IT VEGGIE

Use a plant-based mince.

PORCINI MUSHROOM ALFREDO BAKE

A gorgeous easy pasta bake, comforting and delicious!

Prep: 10 minutes | **Cook:** 1 hour | **Serves:** 4

COOK AHEAD

- 1 tbsp olive oil
- 250g mushrooms, thinly sliced
- 1 tsp chopped garlic
- 50g butter
- ½ cup (50g) plain flour
- 2 cups (500ml) semi-skimmed milk
- ¾ cup (100g) grated Parmesan
- 250g packet of porcini mushroom tortellini
- 210g ball of mozzarella, drained
- salt and pepper

IF MAKING AHEAD FOR THE FRIDGE OR FREEZER

1. Heat the oil in a large, deep-sided frying pan over a medium heat. Add the mushrooms and cook until they have released all their liquid. Once cooked, stir through the garlic, cook for another minute then tip out into a bowl.
2. To the same pan, add the butter and leave to melt. Once melted, whisk in the flour, then slowly pour in the milk a little at a time, whisking the whole time until smooth. Stir through the Parmesan and season with salt and pepper.
3. Stir through the cooked mushrooms and tortellini and tip into a medium ovenproof dish. Tear over the mozzarella.
4. Place a lid on and freeze flat.

OVEN

Preheat the oven to 190°C/170°C fan. Remove the frozen bake from the freezer, take the lid off and cover with foil. Bake in the oven for 1 hour–1 hour 10 minutes, removing the foil after 30 minutes.

AIR FRYER

Remove from the freezer and leave to fully defrost. Once defrosted, preheat the air fryer to 180°C and cook for 30–40 minutes.

IF COOKING NOW

Follow the method for 'if making ahead' until the end of step 3.

OVEN

Preheat the oven to 190°C/170°C fan. Cook in the oven for 20 minutes until golden and bubbly.

Use Italian-style hard cheese instead of Parmesan.

DINNERS

ONE-TRAY SUNDAY LUNCH

Do you love a Sunday roast but hate the faff of making multiple bits? Try my one-tray Sunday lunch – chicken, roasties, veggies and sausages, everything together and cooked in half the time!

Prep: 5 minutes | **Cook:** 35–40 minutes | **Serves:** 4

GRAB AND COOK

- 1kg skin-on chicken thighs
- 6 chipolata sausages
- 10 frozen shop-bought roast potatoes
- 2 carrots, peeled and cut into batons
- 2 parsnips, peeled and cut into batons
- 2 tsp dried rosemary
- 3 tbsp olive oil
- salt and pepper

❄ IF MAKING AHEAD FOR THE FRIDGE OR FREEZER

1. Add the chicken, sausages, roast potatoes, carrots and parsnips to a mixing bowl, sprinkle over the rosemary, olive oil and salt and pepper and toss gently to combine.

2. Add to a large labelled freezer bag, seal and freeze flat.

OVEN

Remove from the freezer and leave to fully defrost. Preheat the oven to 180°C/160°C fan. Pour everything out onto a large casserole dish. Place the chicken thighs on the top and cook for 35–40 minutes until everything is golden.

AIR FRYER

Remove from the freezer and leave to fully defrost. Pour everything out onto a large tray (this cooking method requires a large-drawered air fryer). Place the chicken thighs on the top and cook in the air fryer at 180°C for 25–30 minutes until everything is golden.

🍲 IF COOKING NOW

Follow the method for 'if making ahead' until the end of step 1.

OVEN

Preheat the oven to 180°C/160°C fan. Pour everything out onto a large casserole dish. Place the chicken thighs on the top and cook for 35–40 minutes until everything is golden.

AIR FRYER

Pour everything out onto a large tray (this cooking method requires a large-drawered air fryer). Place the chicken thighs on the top and cook in the air fryer at 180°C for 25–30 minutes until everything is golden.

MAKE IT VEGGIE

Substitute the chicken thighs for quorn chicken fillets and use plant-based chipolatas.

RATATOUILLE-INSPIRED HAKE PARCELS

Want to change up the fish? Any white fish works great in this recipe!

Prep: 5 minutes | **Cook:** 30 minutes | **Serves:** 4

GRAB AND COOK

- 1 courgette, thinly sliced
- 3 large tomatoes, thinly sliced
- 4 hake fillets, skin removed
- 4 tbsp sun-dried tomato pesto
- 8 tbsp breadcrumbs
- ½ cup (70g) grated mozzarella

❄️ IF MAKING AHEAD FOR THE FRIDGE OR FREEZER

1. Cut 4 squares of tin foil roughly 30cm x 30cm in size to make each of the parcels.
2. Arrange the courgette and tomato slices evenly between the foil squares, layering alternately as you go.
3. Place the hake fillets on top of the layered vegetables and spread each one with 1 tablespoon of pesto.
4. Mix the breadcrumbs and cheese in a small bowl and distribute the breadcrumb topping on top of all the fish fillets – the pesto should help the breadcrumbs to stick. Wrap each parcel up carefully.
5. Place into a labelled freezer bag and freeze flat.

OVEN

Preheat the oven to 180°C/160°C fan. Remove the frozen parcels from the freezer bag and place on a baking tray, opening them up slightly at the top. Bake for 30 minutes until the fish is cooked through.

AIR FRYER

Preheat the air fryer to 180°C. Remove the frozen parcels from the freezer bag and place in the air fryer, opening them up slightly at the top. Cook for 25 minutes until the fish is cooked through.

🍲 IF COOKING NOW

Follow the method for 'if making ahead' until the end of step 4.

OVEN

Preheat the oven to 180°C/160°C fan. Place the parcels on a baking tray, open them up slightly at the top and cook for 25 minutes until the fish is cooked through.

AIR FRYER

Preheat the air fryer to 180°C. Place the parcels in the air fryer, open them up slightly at the top and cook for 18–20 minutes until the fish is cooked through.

DINNERS

SAUSAGE TRAYBAKE

This one-tray bake needs nothing more, simply serve as it is!

Prep: 5 minutes | **Cook:** 30–40 minutes | **Serves:** 4

GRAB AND COOK

- 12 chicken chipolata sausages
- 200g cherry tomatoes
- 3 red onions, cut into quarters
- 2 red peppers, sliced into thick chunks
- 1 x 400g tin of cooked potatoes, drained and patted dry
- 3 tbsp olive oil
- 1 tsp dried rosemary
- 1 tsp smoked paprika
- salt and pepper

❄ IF MAKING AHEAD FOR THE FRIDGE OR FREEZER

1. Add everything to a large mixing bowl and mix.
2. Add to a large labelled freezer bag, seal and freeze flat.

OVEN

Remove from the freezer and leave to fully defrost. Preheat the oven to 180°C/160°C fan. Pour everything onto a tray, arranging the chipolatas on top. Cook in the oven for 30–40 minutes until golden.

AIR FRYER

Remove from the freezer and leave to fully defrost. Preheat the air fryer to 180°C. Pour everything onto a tray, arranging the chipolatas on top. Place into the air fryer and cook for 25–30 minutes until golden.

🍲 IF COOKING NOW

Follow the method for 'if making ahead' until the end of step 1.

OVEN

Preheat the oven to 180°C/160°C fan. Pour everything onto a tray, arranging the chipolatas on top. Cook in the oven for 30–40 minutes until golden.

AIR FRYER

Preheat the air fryer to 180°C. Pour everything onto a tray, arranging the chipolatas on top. Place into the air fryer and cook for 25–30 minutes until golden.

MAKE IT VEGGIE

Simply use plant-based sausages.

DINNERS

SPATCHCOCK SUNDAY CHICKEN

A delicious, easy way to enjoy a roast chicken – serve with gravy and some Yorkshire puddings!

Prep: 10 minutes | **Cook:** 1 hour | **Serves:** 4

GRAB AND COOK

- 1 large whole chicken
- 2 tsp dried rosemary
- 1 tsp dried thyme
- 1 tsp garlic purée
- 3 tbsp olive oil
- 400g baby carrots
- 2 onions, diced into chunks
- salt and pepper

❄ IF MAKING AHEAD FOR THE FRIDGE OR FREEZER

1. To spatchcock the chicken, turn it upside down with the legs pointing towards you. Using extra sharp scissors, cut down each side of the backbone, through the ribs and right to the end, then remove the backbone.
2. Turn the chicken back over, skin-side up, and open it out. Using the palm of your hand, push the chicken down firmly so that it flattens.
3. Add the rosemary, thyme, garlic, olive oil and salt and pepper to a bowl and mix. Spread this all over the chicken.
4. Add the carrots and onions to a large labelled freezer bag, then add the chicken and seal. Place in the freezer.

OVEN

Remove from the freezer and leave to fully defrost. Once defrosted, preheat the oven to 190°C/170°C fan, pour the carrots and onions onto a tray, then lay the chicken on top. Cook for 1 hour–1 hour 10 minutes until the chicken is cooked through.

AIR FRYER

Remove from the freezer and leave to fully defrost. Once defrosted, preheat the air fryer to 180°C, pour the carrots and onions onto a tray, then lay the chicken on top. Cook for 50 minutes–1 hour until the chicken is cooked through.

IF COOKING NOW

Follow the method for 'if making ahead' until the end of step 3.

OVEN

Preheat the oven to 190°C/170°C fan, pour the carrots and onions onto a tray, then lay the chicken on top. Cook for 1 hour–1 hour 10 minutes until the chicken is cooked through.

AIR FRYER

Preheat the air fryer to 180°C, pour the carrots and onions onto a tray, then lay the chicken on top. Cook for 50 minutes–1 hour until the chicken is cooked through.

DINNERS

STEAK PIE

Prefer not to have the pastry? Just make the steak pie base and serve with potato and veggies for a beef stew rather than a pie.

Prep: 15 minutes | **Cook:** 3–8 hours | **Serves:** 4

COOK AHEAD

2 tbsp olive oil

1kg beef shin, diced

1 cup (115g) frozen diced onions

2 large carrots, peeled and diced into chunks

1 tbsp tomato purée

2 tbsp plain flour

2½ cups (600ml) beef stock

1 ready-rolled sheet of puff pastry

To cook

1 egg, beaten

❄ IF MAKING AHEAD FOR THE FRIDGE OR FREEZER

1. Heat the oil in a casserole dish over a high heat.
2. Add the beef and brown in batches until golden all over.
3. Remove the beef from the pan and set aside, then add the onions and carrots. Cook for 2–3 minutes, then add the tomato purée and flour and mix.
4. Pour in the beef stock, mix well, then return the browned beef to the pan.
5. Bring to the boil, then transfer to a slow cooker. Cook for 6–8 hours on low until the beef is lovely and tender. Alternatively, place a lid on the casserole dish and cook in the oven at 160°C/140°C fan for 3 hours until the beef is tender.
6. Once cooked, leave to cool then add to a large labelled freezer bag and seal. Freeze flat alongside the puff pastry.

OVEN

Remove from the freezer and leave to fully defrost. Once defrosted, preheat the oven to 180°C/160°C fan. Pour the beef filling into an ovenproof dish and cover with the puff pastry. Trim off the edges of the pastry, brush with beaten egg and bake in the oven for 30–35 minutes until golden.

AIR FRYER

Remove from the freezer and leave to fully defrost. Warm the beef filling in a saucepan on the hob for 5 minutes. Once warmed through, pour into an ovenproof dish and cover with the puff pastry. Trim off the edges of the pastry and brush with beaten egg. Preheat the air fryer to 180°C, then place the pie into the air fryer and bake for 25–30 minutes until golden.

IF COOKING NOW

Follow the method for 'if making ahead' until the end of step 5.

OVEN

Preheat the oven to 180°C/160°C fan. Pour the beef filling into an ovenproof dish and cover with the puff pastry. Trim off the edges of the pastry and brush with beaten egg. Cook in the oven for 30–35 minutes until golden.

AIR FRYER

Pour the beef filling into an ovenproof dish and cover with the puff pastry. Trim off the edges of the pastry and brush with beaten egg. Preheat the air fryer to 180°C, then place the pie inside and cook for 25–30 minutes until golden.

CHEESY HAM STUFFED CHICKEN BREASTS

Serve these delicious stuffed chicken breasts with wedges and salad for an easy meal.

Prep: 5–10 minutes | **Cook:** 20 minutes | **Serves:** 4

GRAB AND COOK

4 skinless chicken breasts

4 tbsp herby cream cheese

4 slices of ham

2 large tomatoes, sliced

240g ball of mozzarella, drained and cut into 8 slices

❄ IF MAKING AHEAD FOR THE FRIDGE OR FREEZER

1. Place the chicken breasts on a chopping board and cut down the side of the chicken breasts to create a pocket, making sure not to cut all the way through.
2. Working with one chicken breast at a time, open the pocket and add 1 tablespoon of cream cheese, 1 slice of ham, some sliced tomato and 2 slices of mozzarella. Fold the pocket over to enclose the filling. Repeat with the remaining chicken breasts.
3. Add to a large labelled freezer bag, seal and freeze flat.

OVEN

Remove from the freezer and leave to fully defrost. Preheat the oven to 180°C/160°C fan. Place the chicken breasts on a lined tray and cook for 25–30 minutes until the chicken is cooked through.

AIR FRYER

Remove from the freezer and leave to fully defrost. Preheat the air fryer to 180°C. Place the chicken breasts on a lined tray and cook for 20–25 minutes until the chicken is cooked through.

IF COOKING NOW

Follow the method for 'if making ahead' until the end of step 2.

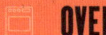 OVEN

Preheat the oven to 180°C/160°C fan. Place the chicken breasts on a lined baking tray and cook for 25–30 minutes until the chicken is cooked through.

AIR FRYER

Preheat the air fryer to 180°C. Place the chicken breasts on a lined tray and cook for 20–25 minutes until the chicken is cooked through.

DINNERS

SWEET AND SOUR CHICKEN

A fakeaway classic!

Prep: 5 minutes | **Cook:** 20 minutes | **Serves:** 4

COOK AHEAD

1 tbsp vegetable oil

4 skinless chicken breasts, cut into chunks

2 tsp garlic purée

2 tsp ginger purée

2 red peppers, diced

2 carrots, peeled and sliced

1 x 400g tin of pineapple chunks in juice, drained

4 tbsp soy sauce

4 tsp cornflour

½ cup (120ml) water

IF MAKING AHEAD FOR THE FRIDGE OR FREEZER

1. Place a frying pan over a medium heat. Add the oil, then add the chicken breasts and cook until brown all over. Add the garlic and ginger purées, peppers and carrots.

2. Add the diced pineapple, soy sauce and cornflour. Stir well, then add the water. Cook for 15 minutes, adding a splash of more water if it looks too thick.

3. Leave to cool, then add to a labelled freezer bag, seal and freeze flat.

HOB

Remove from the freezer and leave to fully defrost. Once defrosted, pour into a saucepan and heat through until piping hot.

MICROWAVE

Remove from the freezer and leave to fully defrost. Pour into a microwave-safe container and reheat for 2–3 minutes until piping hot.

IF COOKING NOW

Follow the method for 'if making ahead' until the end of step 2, then serve with plain or egg fried rice.

DINNERS

SWEETCORN AND SAGE RISOTTO

A delicious oven-baked risotto.

Prep: 10 minutes | **Cook:** 20 minutes | **Serves:** 4–6

COOK AHEAD

5 cups (1.2 litres) vegetable stock

1 x 400g tin of sweetcorn, drained

1 large carrot, peeled and grated

50g butter

1 tsp chopped garlic

1 cup (115g) frozen diced onions

1 tsp dried sage

2 cups (300g) arborio rice

1½ cups (150g) grated Parmesan

salt and pepper

❄ IF MAKING AHEAD FOR THE FRIDGE OR FREEZER

1. Preheat the oven to 180°C/160°C fan. Add the vegetable stock to a large casserole dish or ovenproof saucepan with a lid. Add half of the sweetcorn and the grated carrot, bring to the boil and cook for a couple of minutes. Transfer to a blender and blend till smooth.
2. Melt the butter in the same pan. Once melted, add the chopped garlic and onions and cook until soft. Add the sage and rice, stirring to coat the rice in the onions and butter and then pour in the blended stock and sweetcorn. Bring to the boil, pop a lid on and place into the oven for 18 minutes.
3. Remove from the oven. Mix through the remaining sweetcorn and the Parmesan and season with salt and pepper.
4. Leave to cool, then add to a labelled freezer bag, seal and freeze flat.

HOB

Remove from the freezer and leave to fully defrost. Once defrosted, transfer to a saucepan and heat through over a low heat until piping hot.

MICROWAVE

Remove from the freezer and leave to fully defrost. Once defrosted, heat through in the microwave for 3 minutes, stirring halfway.

IF COOKING NOW

Follow the method for 'if making ahead' until the end of step 3. This is now ready to eat!

MAKE IT VEGGIE

Use Italian-style hard cheese instead of Parmesan.

DINNERS

CONVERSION TABLES

WEIGHTS		VOLUME		OVEN TEMPERATURES			
Metric	Imperial	Metric	Imperial	°C	Fan °C	°F	Gas Mark
15g	½ oz	25ml	1 fl oz	140°C	120°C	275°F	Gas Mark 1
25g	1 oz	50ml	2 fl oz	150°C	130°C	300°F	Gas Mark 2
40g	1½ oz	85ml	3 fl oz	160°C	140°C	325°F	Gas Mark 3
50g	2 oz	150ml	5 fl oz (¼ pint)	180°C	160°C	350°F	Gas Mark 4
75g	3 oz	300ml	10 fl oz (½ pint)	190°C	170°C	375°F	Gas Mark 5
100g	4 oz	450ml	15 fl oz (¾ pint)	200°C	180°C	400°F	Gas Mark 6
150g	5 oz	600ml	1 pint	220°C	200°C	425°F	Gas Mark 7
175g	6 oz	700ml	1¼ pints	230°C	210°C	450°F	Gas Mark 8
200g	7 oz	900ml	1½ pints	240°C	220°C	475°F	Gas Mark 9
225g	8 oz	1 litre	1¾ pints				

MEASUREMENTS

Metric	Imperial	Metric	Imperial
0.5cm	¼ inch	15cm	6 inches
1cm	½ inch	18cm	7 inches
2.5cm	1 inch	20cm	8 inches
5cm	2 inches	23cm	9 inches
7.5cm	3 inches	25cm	10 inches
10cm	4 inches	30cm	12 inches

Weights		Volume	
250g	9 oz	1.2 litres	2 pints
275g	10 oz	1.25 litres	2¼ pints
350g	12 oz	1.5 litres	2½ pints
375g	13 oz	1.6 litres	2¾ pints
400g	14 oz	1.75 litres	3 pints
425g	15 oz	1.8 litres	3¼ pints
450g	1 lb	2 litres	3½ pints
550g	1¼ lb	2.1 litres	3¾ pints
675g	1½ lb	2.25 litres	4 pints
900g	2 lb	2.75 litres	5 pints
1.5kg	3 lb	3.4 litres	6 pints
1.75kg	4 lb	3.9 litres	7 pints
2.25kg	5 lb	5 litres	8 pints (1 gal)

INDEX

A
apple pie overnight oats 48
avocado: scrambled eggs with avocado on toast 49

B
bacon: BLT pasta 62
batch cooking 7–15
    budgeting 16–17
    meal planning 18–19, 23–43
beef
    burgers 92
    mince fajitas 104
    slow-cooked beef massaman 91
    steak pie 116–17
bread, bagels, wraps etc.
    breakfast burritos 55
    chicken caesar baguettes 60
    chicken mayo pittas 60
    French toast 47
    ham, cheese and pesto open bagels 58
    mince fajitas 104
    scrambled eggs with avocado on toast 49
    tortilla pizzas 80
    tuna melt paninis 61
burgers 92
butternut squash soup 71

C
carrots: steak pie 116–17
cheese
    cheese and veggie frittata 67
    cheesy ham stuffed chicken breasts 118
    egg, ham and cheese muffins 65
    Greek rice salad 83
    ham, cheese and pesto open bagels 58
    homemade pizza and calzones 96
    mac and cheese 102
    Mediterranean couscous with halloumi 78
    porcini mushroom alfredo bake 106
    ratatouille-inspired hake parcels 110
    tortilla pizzas 80
    tuna melt paninis 61
chicken
    cheesy ham stuffed chicken breasts 118
    chicken caesar baguettes 60
    chicken korma 94
    chicken mayo and sweetcorn pasta 64
    chicken mayo pittas 60
    chicken noodle soup jars 74
    chicken shawarma skewers 98
    one-tray Sunday lunch 109
    spatchcock Sunday chicken 114
    sweet and sour chicken 120
chickpeas
    hummus 85
    Mediterranean couscous with halloumi 78
courgettes: ratatouille-inspired hake parcels 110
couscous: Mediterranean couscous with halloumi 78
curries
    chicken korma 94
    katsu curry with tofu 101
    slow-cooked beef massaman 91

E
eggs
    breakfast burritos 55
    cheese and veggie frittata 67
    egg fried rice 68
    egg, ham and cheese muffins 65
    fluffy pancakes 46
    French toast 47
    omelette bags 54
    scrambled eggs with avocado on toast 49

F
French toast 47
fruit
    bircher muesli 52
    PBJ smoothie bags 49
    very berry baked oats 53

H
hake: ratatouille-inspired hake parcels 110
ham
    cheesy ham stuffed chicken breasts 118
    egg, ham and cheese muffins 65
    ham, cheese and pesto open bagels 58
    omelette bags 54
    sun-dried tomato orzo pasta 77
hummus 85

M
milk
    fluffy pancakes 46
    PBJ smoothie bags 49
    very berry baked oats 53
muesli: bircher muesli 52

mushrooms
    omelette bags 54
    porcini mushroom alfredo bake 106

N
noodles: chicken noodle soup jars 74

O
oats
    apple pie overnight oats 48
    bircher muesli 52
    very berry baked oats 53
olives: Greek rice salad 83

P
pancakes: fluffy pancakes 46
pasta
    BLT pasta 62
    chicken mayo and sweetcorn pasta 64
    mac and cheese 102
    pesto orzo salad 77
    pizza pasta salad 80
    porcini mushroom alfredo bake 106
    sun-dried tomato orzo pasta 77
    tuna, sweetcorn and spring onion pasta salad 76
peanut butter: PBJ smoothie bags 49
peas: cheese and veggie frittata 67
peppers
    cheese and veggie frittata 67
    omelette bags 54
    sweet and sour chicken 120
pies: steak pie 116–17
pineapple: sweet and sour chicken 120
pizza
    homemade pizza and calzones 96
    tortilla pizzas 80
potatoes
    freezable baked potatoes 84
    one-tray Sunday lunch 109
    sausage traybake 112

R
rice
    egg fried rice 68
    Greek rice salad 83
    sweetcorn and sage risotto 122

S
salads
    Greek rice salad 83
    Mediterranean couscous with halloumi 78
    pesto orzo salad 77
    pizza pasta salad 80
    tuna, sweetcorn and spring onion pasta salad 76

salami: pizza pasta salad 80
sausages
    breakfast burritos 55
    sausage traybake 112
skewers: chicken shawarma skewers 98
smoothies: PBJ smoothie bags 49
soup
    butternut squash soup 71
    chicken noodle soup jars 74
    chunky vegetable soup 73
    tomato and basil soup 72
sweet potatoes
    chicken korma 94
    slow-cooked beef massaman 91
sweetcorn
    chicken mayo and sweetcorn pasta 64
    sweetcorn and sage risotto 122
    tuna, sweetcorn and spring onion pasta salad 76

T
tofu: katsu curry with tofu 101
tomatoes
    5-a-day pasta sauce 88
    BLT pasta 62
    chicken mayo pittas 60
    homemade pizza and calzones 96
    omelette bags 54
    pizza pasta salad 80
    ratatouille-inspired hake parcels 110
    sun-dried tomato orzo pasta 77
    tomato and basil soup 72
tuna
    tuna melt paninis 61
    tuna, sweetcorn and spring onion pasta salad 76

V
vegetables, mixed
    5-a-day pasta sauce 88
    chicken korma 94
    chunky vegetable soup 73
    egg fried rice 68
    one-tray Sunday lunch 109
    sausage traybake 112

Y
yoghurt
    apple pie overnight oats 48
    bircher muesli 52

THANKS

Batch from Scratch has been an absolute joy to bring to life, from screen to page! This book is a continuation of everything I love about simple, practical cooking, and it's been such an exciting adventure turning the TV show into something you can hold in your hands, scribble notes in and cook from again and again.

First and foremost, a huge thank you to the incredible team at Ebury, Penguin, for once again helping me shape my ideas into a finished book. A huge thank you to the whole team – Stephanie Milner, Rosie Pearce, Abby Watson, Francesca Thomson, Lucy Harrison and everyone else behind the scenes – your support and belief in my vision never wavers.

A massive thank you goes to the *Batch from Scratch* TV production company Southshore Productions, who brought the show to life with such energy, creativity and care. Being on set was a whole new experience for me and I've learned so much, so a huge thank you to the on-location production crew and the Southshore team in the London and Cardiff offices.

A huge thanks to Lidl for sponsoring the show – we have worked together for many years and without your sponsorship this show wouldn't have made it to TV, and for that I'm very grateful. It always a pleasure working with Team Lidl!

To my wonderful co-presenter Joe Swash, thank you for bringing so much energy, humour and kindness to the show. You always make me laugh, keep me calm when I need it and are endlessly patient when I forget my lines. I've learnt so much from working with you – and had a great time doing it!

To Andrew Hayes-Watkins, thank you for the great photography. Once again, you've made the photography process not just painless, but *fun*! To Pippa Leon for food styling and Megan Thomson for props, thank you for making these simple recipes look so high-end.

To my amazing team at Curtis Brown Group, thank you for being by my side across both publishing and TV. To Cathryn Summerhayes, thank you for guiding me through another year of exciting changes. To Martha Atack and Emily Harris, thank you for your incredible support on the TV side – it's been a whole new world and I've loved every minute of it. I'm so lucky to have you all in my corner.

To my lovely assistant Nicola Bruce, what can I say? We may be a team of two, but we've got the energy of ten! Thank you for being by my side through every twist and turn, from batch recipes to broadcast schedules. Your commitment, patience and hard work mean the world.

To my family, you're my everything, thank you for sharing me with Batch Lady life! And to my followers and the watchers of *Batch from Scratch*, thank you for viewing and joining in on the batching journey.

Suzanne x

EBURY PRESS

UK | USA | Canada | Ireland | Australia
India | New Zealand | South Africa

Ebury Press is part of the Penguin Random House group of companies whose addresses can be found at global.penguinrandomhouse.com

Penguin Random House UK
One Embassy Gardens, 8 Viaduct Gardens, London SW11 7BW

penguin.co.uk
global.penguinrandomhouse.com

First published by Ebury Press in 2026

2

Copyright © Suzanne Mulholland 2026
Photography © Andrew Hayes-Watkins 2026

The moral right of the author has been asserted.

No part of this book may be used or reproduced in any manner for the purpose of training artificial intelligence technologies or systems. In accordance with Article 4(3) of the DSM Directive 2019/790, Penguin Random House expressly reserves this work from the text and data mining exception.

Publishing Director: Stephanie Milner
Senior Editor: Rosie Pearce
Senior Production Manager: Lucy Harrison
Cover Designer: Shasmin Mozomil based on *Batch from Scratch* Channel 4 TV show design
Interior Designer: maru studio G.K. based on design by Studio Nic&Lou
Photographer: Andrew Hayes-Watkins
Food Stylist: Pippa Leon
Prop Stylist: Megan Thomson

Colour origination by Altaimage Ltd
Printed and bound in Italy by LEGO SpA

The authorised representative in the EEA is Penguin Random House Ireland, Morrison Chambers, 32 Nassau Street, Dublin D02 YH68.

A CIP catalogue record for this book is available from the British Library

ISBN 9781529986655

Penguin Random House is committed to a sustainable future for our business, our readers and our planet. This book is made from Forest Stewardship Council® certified paper.